WILLY RUSSELL

Blood Brothers

With an Introduction and Teaching Notes by
JIM MULLIGAN

BLOOMSBURY
NEW DELHI • LONDON • OXFORD • NEW YORK • SYDNEY

First published in India 2017
First published in Great Britain in this edition in 1995 by Methuen Drama
Reprinted by Bloomsbury Methuen Drama 2012, 2013 (twice), 2014, 2015
(three times), 2016 (four times)

Blood Brothers first published in a collection with *Educating Rita* and
Stags and Hens in 1986 by Methuen London Ltd

Bloomsbury Methuen Drama
An imprint of Bloomsbury Publishing Plc
Imprint previously known as Methuen Drama

BLOOMSBURY, METHUEN DRAMA and
the Diana logo are trademarks of Bloomsbury Publishing Plc
This edition published with permission from Bloomsbury Publishing Plc
50 Bedford Square, London WC1B 3DP

British Library Cataloguing-in-Publication Data
A catalogue record for this book is available from the British Library.
Library of Congress Cataloging-in-Publication Data
A catalog record for this book is available from the Library of Congress.

ISBN: 978 93 86349 09 5
10 9 8 7 6 5 4 3 2 1
For sale in the Indian subcontinent only

Bloomsbury Publishing India Pvt. Ltd
Second Floor, Building No. 4
DDA Complex LSC, Pocket C – 6 & 7
Vasant Kunj, New Delhi 110070
www.bloomsbury.com

Series: Student Editions

Printed and bound in India by Thomson Press India Ltd.

Contents

Willy Russell

1947 Born in Whiston, just outside Liverpool.
1962 Leaves school to become a ladies' hairdresser.
1969 Returns to education as a mature student.
1972 *Blind Scouse* is premièred at the Edinburgh Festival.
1973 *When the Reds*, an adaptation of Alan Plater's work, is presented in Liverpool.
King of the Castle is shown on BBC1.
1974 *John, Paul, George, Ringo . . . and Bert* wins the Evening Standard and London Theatre Critics' Award for Best Musical.
1975 *Breezeblock Park* opens at the Everyman Theatre, Liverpool, transfers to the Mermaid Theatre, London (1977) and then to the Whitehall Theatre.
Break-In is shown on BBC1.
Death of a Young Young Man is shown on BBC2.
1976 *One for the Road* opens at the Contact Theatre, Manchester. Subsequently at the Lyric Theatre, London.
Our Day Out is shown on BBC1 and subsequently adapted for the stage.
1978 *The Daughters of Albion* is shown on ITV.
Stags and Hens, originally a student piece for Manchester Polytechnic, opens at the Everyman Theatre, Liverpool.
1979 *Lies* is shown on BBC1.
1980 *Educating Rita* is commissioned by the Royal Shakespeare Company and given London's SWET Award for Best Comedy.
The Boy with the Transistor Radio is commissioned and shown by ITV.
1981 Writes the screenplay for *Educating Rita*, which is made into a film starring Michael Caine and Julie Walters. The screenplay is nominated for an Academy Award.

1983 *Blood Brothers* opens in Liverpool and moves to London.
Awarded an Honorary M.A. by the Open University.
One Summer is shown on Channel 4.

1988 Bill Kenwright opens a new West End production of *Blood Brothers*.

1989 *Shirley Valentine* is a nominee for the Tony Award and Drama Desk Award for Best Play and wins the Olivier Award for Best Comedy of the Year.

1990 Writes screenplay for *Dancing thru' the Dark*, based on *Stags and Hens*.
Writes the screenplay for *Shirley Valentine* and the film is produced starring Pauline Collins, directed by Lewis Gilbert.
Made a Doctor of Letters by Liverpool University.

1993 *Terraces*, an early work, is revived by Scene Drama and shown on BBC1.
Blood Brothers opens on Broadway.

Introduction

First night on a November afternoon

Blood Brothers was first performed in a secondary school in Fazakerly, a suburb of Liverpool, in 1982. It was a memorable first night even though it took place on a November afternoon before an audience of four hundred children. There were minimal props, a minimal set and no scenery. Nor was there any music. Willy Russell recalls:

> The Merseyside Young People's Theatre Company used to bring plays to the schools in order to give the kids an experience of theatre without any hidden or overt agenda and they asked me to write a play for them. I'd had the idea of *Blood Brothers* for years but had never got around to writing it so I took this chance. We had no trickery or theatre technology to hide behind. We had a good story and we had to tell it and grab the most difficult audience in the world. Kids like that believe that if you've been arrogant enough to stand up in front of them and perform a play it had better be good. If it isn't they'll switch off.

From this beginning the play developed until now it is translated into at least ten languages and is performed regularly all over the world.

A story that came out of the blue

> The story sounds as if it is a Greek myth but there is no existing story, as far as I know, about twins secretly parted who then end up killed on the day they learn the truth about themselves. It feels as if it's a story that's always existed and that's what I wanted to create. But in fact I was walking along one day and didn't have an idea of the story, then I took the next step and I had it. It just came out of the blue. The whole story was there. It was one of

> those moments that make you want to put your hands together and thank whoever it is you believe in for sending it to you.

One song leads to seven others

Years before *Blood Brothers* Willy Russell had performed as a singer-songwriter in clubs and pubs while he was working during the day as a ladies' hairdresser.

> I left school with two things: English Language O-level and the conviction that I would never work in a factory. At the back of my mind was the notion that I could be a writer. The performing started one night in The Spinners Club where they used to have a floor spot for anyone to perform their own songs. Unbeknownst to me, my mate had put me down and the next thing I knew I was up on stage singing a song I had written about the Kirkby Estate. It was an out-of-the-body experience. On one level I could feel my knees knocking and on another level I could hear gales of laughter. So the comic song I had written was working. I loved it – not the fact that I had performed well but that the song I had written had been a success. The next week I was there with seven more songs.

The life that lets you stay younger longer

Willy Russell carried on like this for a number of years writing in the hairdressing shop when things were slack and gradually becoming aware of other influences. He read more widely and mixed with students until Annie, a student friend who later became his wife, suggested he should take English Literature O-level. Willy realised that at one subject a year he would never make it so he left hairdressing and spent a year studying for O- and A-levels so that he could go to college.

> I really had no idea about student life. I just thought college was like school and then I found these students sitting on beautiful green lawns in summer and I couldn't

believe young people could live like this. It's a life that allows you to stay younger longer and I wanted some of it. So I worked at it and made it.

The women's view of the world seeped into me from an early age

Willy Russell is not a reticent person but he does not see why personal details about his life should be relevant to an understanding of his plays. He is, however, prepared to explore some of his early influences. Why, for example, should a man who grew up in working-class Liverpool, notorious as a male-dominated society, write so effectively about women who have dignity, strength and the resilience to fight off the sexism of a male-dominated society?

For one thing it is a dramatist's job to convince an audience and if I decide to write about Shirley Valentine or Rita or Mrs Johnstone it is my job to make it convincing. But I would be deluding myself if I thought it was only that. I have never wanted to write autobiography in my plays yet when I look at *Educating Rita* I see that it is glaringly autobiographical. Maybe I chose to work through women because I wanted to get to the *truth* about myself rather than the facts of the matter. Remember I wrote *Shirley Valentine* when I was approaching forty. If you look at some of the things *Shirley Valentine* addresses they were the things I was concerned with. My hair was going grey, certain joints were starting to ache and the ageing process was starting to bother me, but men don't have the language to discuss these matters and women do. Perhaps it was easier for me to tell about these things using a woman's voice. Having said all that I think it cannot be denied that as a child I was deeply influenced by women. I was brought up on an estate of 350 houses that had been put up during the war to house munitions workers. Both my aunts and my grandmother lived within 500 yards of my mother. And, since all the men were on shift work, the women – my mother, Dolly and Edna – would gather at my grandmother's and I would be there, playing unnoticed in the kitchen. I think that when you are a toddler, women tend to be unguarded. They will talk about things they don't think a four-year-old will take in. They'll undress in front of a child and talk about intimate things that they would never mention to men, so it may well be that the women's view of the world seeped into my pores from a very early age. And it could be significant that I was a ladies' hairdresser for six years.

Brought up to see both sides of the question

Blood Brothers is based upon the premise that the class you belong to will, to a large extent, determine your life chances. Willy Russell accepts that belonging to the working class does not inevitably lead to socialism – otherwise how could you explain working-class Tories or racists – but he is clear about the pressures on members of his class and the influence of his parents.

I was brought up as a member of a class whose members were treated like second-class citizens. I was aware from a very early age of the injustice of it. We were the ones who went into the mines and factories, who did the manual labour, whose sensitivities were blunted, whose intelligence was never acknowledged. I lived in an environment where we were told every day of our lives that we were thick, daft, stupid and unworthy. My father had been a miner and then worked for ICI. He was not a party member or a tub-thumping socialist but he was very firmly on the side of the underdog. He'd often bring home people who were not waifs and strays exactly but people who had suffered some kind of misfortune. My dad gravitated towards interesting talkers and he liked nothing better on a Saturday night than to have a heated discussion with three or four people on politics or religion. He was part of that socialist tradition. At eighteen he went to night school because he knew he had never learned much at school and in fact he became a very good mathematician. Like many people of his generation his life would have been fantastically different if he'd been born

> into my generation or into a different class, which is what *Blood Brothers* is about. In his situation you knew that people of lesser intelligence, humanity and sensitivity would be controlling your life. My mother was slightly different. She had a great natural sympathy and aspirations. She liked nice things, delicate things which my father distrusted. She realised that refinement and taste had nothing to do with class whereas my father thought they were posh or bourgeois. Both my parents were passionately opposed to mob culture or mob thought. They could never stand unquestioning groups of people and I was brought up to see both sides of a question.

Tea or champagne

In 1969 Willy Russell left hairdressing to work for a year in the warehouse of a factory to raise money for college. Here he saw the class divide at its most pernicious. He worked a forty-hour week in a room with the windows painted black so that the workers would not be distracted. He recalls that every day as the workers took a ten-minute tea break the managing director and his associates would be served champagne with crystal glasses on a silver tray.

> I didn't object to them having champagne but I did object to the insensitivity of them having it served by a waiter who walked past us every afternoon. And back in the factory we would treat each other brutally. The foreman, himself a member of the working class, behaved like an animal because he had a little bit of power and he wanted to satisfy the people over there with the champagne. And we taunted each other in a vicious way. I thought I'd left animalistic behaviour behind me in the playground but it was there lurking in us.

Capable of extreme violence

Willy Russell was not an aggressive child but he liked rough-and-tumble in the playground and team games. He recalls only once playing with a gun, when he was about four, and even then he got into trouble because he had 'robbed' it from the kid next door. In view of the many references to guns in *Blood Brothers* and to the bloody fatal outcome it is interesting to note Willy Russell's attitude to toy guns. Could he be suggesting that Sammy's fascination with toy guns led in some way to his use of a real gun later on?

> All right there are a lot of guns in *Blood Brothers* but they are only make-believe except for the gun Sammy brings in and the guns of the police at the end. And remember there is a fantasy where the whole thing escalates from a cowboy drawing a bead on a rival to a professor letting off an atom bomb. Personally, I detest guns and the dreadful things that people do with them but that doesn't mean I believe children should be prevented from playing with them. I wouldn't deny children that right. I don't celebrate it or share their enjoyment but I allow them the space to play in this way. I would go further and say that this mimetic acting out of aggression with symbolic weaponry has a beneficial effect on society. At least I would need hard evidence that banning toy guns would serve any useful purpose. I accept that children are capable of extreme violence and are potentially brutal but it is how society deals with this that is crucial. I am just not convinced that banning toy guns will do anything towards curbing this aggression in children.

The effortless process that can be agony

Willy Russell has used words like torture, agony, terror and sleepless nights when describing the writing process but he is careful not to overdo what he sees as irrelevant to an audience. It is of no interest to them that he may have struggled to create an effect.

> You do have sleepless nights but you don't go on about it. In fact there's nothing better when you put a play on the stage than for the audience to think that anybody could do it, that the process is effortless. I work in a systematic

way. When I've dropped off the children to school or college I go to the office, a Georgian house a little distance from the centre of Liverpool. Jane will make a cup of tea and we will go over the outstanding phone calls and have a look through the mail. We deal with urgent letters, then I'll ask her to fillet all the phone calls leaving only those from my immediate family or my agent, and then I go up to the attic where I work, switch on the word-processor and pick up where I left off the previous evening. Sometimes I spend days without adding a new syllable and sometimes I'm undoing previous work. If it's a good day I'll work steadily until I have a break for lunch and then it's on until five or six o'clock. If there's nothing I need to do at home I'll go upstairs and work till about ten. And then I switch off. I never drink alcohol or listen to music when I'm working because I think both those things seduce you into thinking that the feelings engendered by the wine or music are present in your work. I will keep this routine up until I have finished a piece of work. This might last for six months but once the work is done then I can relax and go on holiday. I get terribly frustrated if I have to take a break with something unfinished.

The story sent shivers up my spine

Blood Brothers evolved for about eight years before Willy Russell was ready to commit himself to it. Plays like *Shirley Valentine* and *Educating Rita* start with a character and the plot follows but with *Blood Brothers* the whole story was there and the characters had to be invented to inhabit the story.

The story itself sent shivers up my spine so I worried about getting it wrong but, after the shortened version without music, I knew I was ready for the full length musical version. I never deliver a script unless it's complete and playable. I may then get heavily involved in rewriting but I don't expect actors and directors to do my job for me. I always envisioned the children being played by adults. I'd seen plays by John McGrath and Peter Terson in the

> sixties when twenty-year-old men played five-year-old boys with totally acceptable realism. And this was a long time before Dennis Potter used the technique so well in *Blue Remembered Hills*. I also wanted this to have a fairy-tale quality and to achieve this I gave the narrator the rhythms and patterns of the traditional ballads I had sung in the clubs. Bob Swash produced the play for the Liverpool Playhouse with Chris Bond, himself a writer, as director. Chris tended to be over-reverential with the text. He didn't want to cut anything so the play opened in Liverpool with fifteen minutes at the end of Act Two that I felt should be cut. It was dotting the 'i's when the audience didn't need it so, after three months in Liverpool, I took the scissors to that bit before it opened in London. I haven't rewritten anything since then apart from a small change in the North American production to make a little point clear about what re-housing in council property means.

The business of show business

Willy Russell is clear that show business is a business and that he has a superb agent in Tom Erhardt.

> These things have to be managed. There's a lot of tacky stuff that has to be dealt with to make the make-believe work. I feel very honoured and slightly awed by the success of *Blood Brothers*. It's a bit like that first song I sang in The Spinners. I'm delighted the audience accepts what I have written. I'm also, it must be said, slightly bored by the play. I get lots of invitations from directors who want me to see their production and although that is very flattering I am conscious that I have watched the play thousands of times so it is difficult for me to be captivated by it. The last time I saw it in New York I kept looking for flaws and ways to improve it. Then I thought – don't start trying to rewrite this one. It's fine. Leave it alone. Perhaps it's time to write another musical. I will do, if I'm walking along and another idea comes out of the blue into my head. Till then I will do plays without music and keep on

> working at the novel which is occupying me at the moment.

Meanwhile, all over the world audiences are being asked the question

> And do we blame superstition for what came to pass?
> Or could it be what we, the English, have come to know as class?

BLOOD BROTHERS
A Musical

Blood Brothers was first performed at the Liverpool Playhouse on 8 January, 1983, with the following cast:

MRS JOHNSTONE (*Mother*)	Barbara Dickson
MICKEY	George Costigan
EDDIE	Andrew C. Wadsworth
SAMMY	Peter Christian
LINDA	Amanda York
MRS LYONS	Wendy Murray
MR LYONS	Alan Leith
NARRATOR	Andrew Schofield
CHORUS	Hazel Ellerby
	Eithne Brown
	David Edge

Directed by Chris Bond
Designed by Andy Greenfield
Musical Director Peter Filleul
(Presented by arrangement with Bob Swash)

Blood Brothers was subsequently presented by Bob Swash, by arrangement with Liverpool Playhouse at the Lyric Theatre, London, on 11 April, 1983, with the following cast:

MRS JOHNSTONE (*Mother*)	Barbara Dickson
MICKEY	George Costigan
EDDIE	Andrew C. Wadsworth
SAMMY	Peter Christian
LINDA	Kate Fitzgerald
MRS LYONS	Wendy Murray
MR LYONS	Alan Leith
NARRATOR	Andrew Schofield
CHORUS	Hazel Ellerby
	David Edge
	Ian Burns
	Oliver Beamish

Directed by Chris Bond and Danny Hiller
Designed by Andy Greenfield
Musical Director Richard Spanswick

PRODUCTION NOTE

The setting for *Blood Brothers* is an open stage, with the different settings and time spans being indicated by lighting changes, with the minimum of properties and furniture. The whole play should flow along easily and smoothly, with no cumbersome scene changes. Two areas are semi-permanent – the Lyons house and the Johnstone house. We see the interior of the Lyons' comfortable home but usually only the exterior front door of the Johnstone house, with the 'interior' scenes taking place outside the door. The area between the two houses acts as communal ground for street scenes, park scenes etc.

ACT ONE

The Overture comes to a close.

MRS JOHNSTONE (*singing*): Tell me it's not true
Say it's just a story.

The NARRATOR *steps forward.*

NARRATOR (*speaking*): So did y' hear the story of the Johnstone twins?
As like each other as two new pins,
Of one womb born, on the self same day,
How one was kept and one given away?

An' did you never hear how the Johnstones died,
Never knowing that they shared one name,
Till the day they died, when a mother cried
My own dear sons lie slain.

The Lights come up to show a re-enactment of the final moments of the play – the deaths of MICKEY *and* EDWARD. *The scene fades.*

MRS JOHNSTONE *enters with her back to the audience.*

An' did y' never hear of the mother, so cruel,
There's a stone in place of her heart?
Then bring her on and come judge for yourselves
How she came to play this part.

The NARRATOR *exits.*

Music is heard as MRS JOHNSTONE *turns and walks towards us. She is aged thirty but looks more like fifty.*

MRS JOHNSTONE (*singing*): Once I had a husband,
You know the sort of chap,
I met him at a dance and how he came on with the chat.
He said my eyes were deep blue pools,
My skin as soft as snow,
He told me I was sexier than Marilyn Monroe.

And we went dancing,
We went dancing.

Then, of course, I found
That I was six weeks overdue.
We got married at the registry an' then we had a 'do'.
We all had curly salmon sandwiches,
An' how the ale did flow,
They said the bride was lovelier than Marilyn Monroe.

And we went dancing,
Yes, we went dancing.

Then the baby came along,
We called him Darren Wayne,
Then three months on I found that I was in the club again.
An' though I still fancied dancing,
My husband wouldn't go,
With a wife he said was twice the size of Marilyn Monroe.

No more dancing
No more dancing.

By the time I was twenty-five,
I looked like forty-two,
With seven hungry mouths to feed and one more nearly due.
Me husband, he'd walked out on me,
A month or two ago,
For a girl they say who looks a bit like Marilyn Monroe.

And they go dancing
They go dancing

Yes they go dancing
They go . . .

An irate MILKMAN *(the* NARRATOR*) rushes in to rudely interrupt the song.*

MILKMAN: Listen love, I'm up to here with hard luck stories; you own me three pounds, seventeen and fourpence an' either you pay up today, like now, or I'll be forced to cut off your deliveries.

MRS JOHNSTONE: I said, I said, look, next week I'll pay y' . . .

MILKMAN: Next week, next week! Next week never arrives around here. I'd be a rich man if next week ever came.

MRS JOHNSTONE: But look, look, I start a job next week. I'll have money comin' in an' I'll be able to pay y'. Y' can't stop the milk. I need the milk. I'm pregnant.

MILKMAN: Well, don't look at me, love. I might be a milkman but it's got nothin' to do with me. Now you've been told, no money, no milk.

The MILKMAN *exits.*

MRS JOHNSTONE *stands alone and we hear some of her kids, off.*

KID ONE (*off*): Mam, Mam the baby's cryin'. He wants his bottle. Where's the milk?

KID TWO (*off*): 'Ey Mam, how come I'm on free dinners? All the other kids laugh at me.

KID THREE (*off*): 'Ey Mother, I'm starvin' an' there's nothin' in. There never bloody well is.

MRS JOHNSTONE (*perfunctorily*): Don't swear, I've told y'.

KID FOUR (*off*): Mum, I can't sleep, I'm hungry, I'm starvin' . . .

KIDS (*off*): An' me, Mam. An' me. An' me.

MRS JOHNSTONE (*singing*): I know it's hard on all you kids,
But try and get some sleep.
Next week I'll be earnin',
We'll have loads of things to eat,
We'll have ham, an' jam, an' spam an'

(*Speaking.*) Roast Beef, Yorkshire Puddin', Battenberg Cake, Chicken an' Chips, Corned Beef, Sausages, Treacle Tart, Mince an' Spuds, Milk Shake for the Baby:

There is a chorus of groaning ecstasy from the KIDS.

MRS JOHNSTONE *picks up the tune again.*

When I bring home the dough,
We'll live like kings, like bright young things,
Like Marilyn Monroe.

And we'll go dancing . . .

MRS JOHNSTONE *hums a few bars of the song, and dances a few steps, as she makes her way to her place of work –* MRS LYONS' *house. During the dance she acquires a brush, dusters and a mop bucket.*

MRS LYONS' *house where* MRS JOHNSTONE *is working.*

MRS LYONS *enters, carrying a parcel.*

MRS LYONS: Hello, Mrs Johnstone, how are you? Is the job working out all right for you?

MRS JOHNSTONE: It's, erm, great. Thank you. It's such a lovely house it's a pleasure to clean it.

MRS LYONS: It's a pretty house isn't it? It's a pity it's so big. I'm finding it rather large at present.

MRS JOHNSTONE: Oh. Yeh. With Mr Lyons being away an' that? When does he come back, Mrs Lyons?

MRS LYONS: Oh, it seems such a long time. The Company sent him out there for nine months, so, what's that, he'll be back in about five months' time.

MRS JOHNSTONE: Ah, you'll be glad when he's back won't you? The house won't feel so empty then, will it?

MRS LYONS *begins to unwrap her parcel.*

MRS LYONS: Actually, Mrs J, we bought such a large house for the – for the children – we thought children would come along.

MRS JOHNSTONE: Well y' might still be able to . . .

MRS LYONS: No, I'm afraid . . . We've been trying for such a long time now . . . I wanted to adopt but . . . Mr Lyons is . . well he says he wanted his own son, not someone else's. Myself, I believe that an adopted child can become one's own.

MRS JOHNSTONE: Ah yeh . . . yeh. Ey, it's weird though, isn't it. Here's you can't have kids, an' me, I can't stop havin' them. Me husband used to say that all we had to do was shake hands and I'd be in the club. He must have shook hands with me before he left. I'm havin' another one y' know.

MRS LYONS: Oh, I see . . .

MRS JOHNSTONE: Oh but look, look it's all right, Mrs Lyons, I'll still be able to do me work. Havin' babies, it's like clockwork to me. I'm back on me feet an' workin' the next day y' know. If I have this one at the weekend I won't even need to take one day off. I love this job, y' know. We can just manage to get by now –

She is stopped by MRS LYONS *putting the contents of the package, a pair of new shoes, on to the table.*

Jesus Christ, Mrs Lyons, what are y' trying to do?

MRS LYONS: My God, what's wrong?

MRS JOHNSTONE: The shoes . . . the shoes . . .

MRS LYONS: Pardon?

MRS JOHNSTONE: New shoes on the table, take them off . . .

MRS LYONS *does so.*

(*Relieved*) Oh God, Mrs Lyons, never put new shoes on a table . . . You never know what'll happen.

MRS LYONS (*twigging it; laughing*): Oh . . . you mean you're superstitious?

MRS JOHNSTONE: No, but you never put new shoes on the table.

MRS LYONS: Oh go on with you. Look, if it will make you any happier I'll put them away . . .

MRS LYONS *exits with the shoes.*

Music is heard as MRS JOHNSTONE *warily approaches the table and the* NARRATOR *enters.*

NARRATOR: There's shoes upon the table an' a joker in the pack,
The salt's been spilled and a looking glass cracked,
There's one lone magpie overhead.

MRS JOHNSTONE: I'm not superstitious.

NARRATOR: The Mother said

MRS JOHNSTONE: I'm not superstitious.

NARRATOR: The Mother said.

The NARRATOR *exits to re-enter as a* GYNAECOLOGIST.

MRS JOHNSTONE: What are you doin' here? The milk bill's not due 'till Thursday.

GYNAECOLOGIST (*producing a listening funnel*): Actually I've given up the milk round and gone into medicine. I'm your gynaecologist. (*He begins to examine her.*) OK, Mummy, let's have a little listen to the baby's ticker, shall we?

MRS JOHNSTONE: I was dead worried about havin' another baby, you know, Doctor. I didn't see how we were gonna manage with another mouth to feed. But now I've got me a little job we'll be OK. If I'm careful we can just scrape by, even with another mouth to feed.

The GYNAECOLOGIST *completes his examination.*

GYNAECOLOGIST: Mouths, Mummy.

MRS JOHNSTONE: What?

GYNAECOLOGIST: Plural, Mrs Johnstone. Mouths to feed. You're expecting twins. Congratulations. And the next one please, Nurse.

The GYNAECOLOGIST *exits.*

MRS JOHNSTONE, *numbed by the news, moves back to her work, dusting the table upon which the shoes had been placed.*

MRS LYONS *enters.*

MRS LYONS: Hello, Mrs. J. How are you?

There is no reply.

(*Registering the silence*) Mrs J? Anything wrong?

MRS JOHNSTONE: I had it all worked out.

MRS LYONS: What's the matter?

MRS JOHNSTONE: We were just getting straight.

MRS LYONS: Why don't you sit down.

MRS JOHNSTONE: With one more baby we could have managed. But not with two. The Welfare have already been on to me. They say I'm incapable of controllin' the kids I've already got. They say I should put some of them into care. But I won't. I love the bones of every one of them. I'll even love these two when they come along. But like they say at the Welfare, kids can't live on love alone.

MRS LYONS: Twins? You're expecting twins?

The NARRATOR *enters.*

NARRATOR: How quickly an idea, planted, can
Take root and grow into a plan.
The thought conceived in this very room
Grew as surely as a seed, in a mother's womb.

The NARRATOR *exits.*

MRS LYONS (*almost inaudibly*): Give one to me.

MRS JOHNSTONE: What?

MRS LYONS (*containing her excitement*): Give one of them to me.

MRS JOHNSTONE: Give one to you?

MRS LYONS: Yes . . . yes.

MRS JOHNSTONE (*taking it almost as a joke*): But y' can't just . . .

MRS LYONS: When are you due?

MRS JOHNSTONE: Erm, well about . . . Oh, but Mrs . . .

MRS LYONS: Quickly, quickly tell me . . . when are you due?

MRS JOHNSTONE: July he said, the beginning of . . .

MRS LYONS: July . . . and my husband doesn't get back until, the middle of July. He need never guess . . .

MRS JOHNSTONE (*amused*): Oh, it's mad . . .

MRS LYONS: I know, it is. It's mad . . . but it's wonderful, it's perfect. Look, look, you're what, four months pregnant, but you're only just beginning to show . . . so, so I'm four months pregnant and I'm only just beginning to show. (*She grabs a cushion and arranges it beneath her dress.*) Look, look. I could have got pregnant just before he went away. But I didn't tell him in case I miscarried, I didn't want to worry him whilst he was away. But when he arrives home I tell him we were wrong, the doctors were wrong. I have a baby, our baby. Mrs Johnstone, it will work, it will if only you'll . . .

MRS JOHNSTONE: Oh, Mrs Lyons, you can't be serious.

MRS LYONS: You said yourself, you said you had too many children already.

MRS JOHNSTONE: Yeh, but I don't know if I wanna give one away.

MRS LYONS: Already you're being threatened by the Welfare people. Mrs Johnstone, with two more children how can you possibly avoid some of them being put into care? Surely, it's better to give one child to me. Look, at least if the child was with me you'd be able to see him every day, as you came to work.

MRS LYONS *stares at* MRS JOHNSTONE, *willing her to agree.*

Please, Mrs Johnstone. Please.

MRS JOHNSTONE: Are y' . . . are y' that desperate to have a baby?

MRS LYONS (*singing*): Each day I look out from this window,
I see him with his friends, I hear him call,
I rush down but as I fold my arms around him,
He's gone. Was he ever there at all?

I've dreamed of all the places I would take him,
The games we'd play the stories I would tell,
The jokes we'd share, the clothing I would make him,
I reach out. But as I do. He fades away.

The melody shifts into that of MRS JOHNSTONE *who is looking at* MRS LYONS, *feeling for her.* MRS LYONS *gives a half smile and a shrug, perhaps slightly embarrassed at what she has revealed.* MRS JOHNSTONE *turns and looks at the room she is in. Looking up in awe at the comparative opulence and ease of the place. Tentatively and wondering she sings*

MRS JOHNSTONE: If my child was raised
In a palace like this one,
(He) wouldn't have to worry where
His next meal was comin' from.
His clothing would be (supplied by)
George Henry Lee.

MRS LYONS *sees that* MRS JOHNSTONE *might be persuaded.*

MRS LYONS (*singing*): He'd have all his own toys
And a garden to play in.

MRS JOHNSTONE: He could make too much noise
Without the neighbours complainin'.

MRS LYONS: Silver trays to take meals on

MRS JOHNSTONE: A bike with *both* wheels on?

MRS LYONS *nods enthusiastically.*

MRS LYONS: And he'd sleep every night
In a bed of his own.

MRS JOHNSTONE: He wouldn't get into fights
He'd leave matches alone.
And you'd never find him
Effin' and blindin'.

And when he grew up
He could never be told
To stand and queue up
For hours on end at the dole
He'd grow up to be

MRS LYONS
MRS JOHNSTONE } (*together*): A credit to me

MRS JOHNSTONE: To you.

MRS JOHNSTONE: I would still be able to see him every day, wouldn't I?

MRS LYONS: Of course.

MRS JOHNSTONE: An' . . . an' you would look after him, wouldn't y'?

MRS LYONS (*singing*): I'd keep him warm in the winter
And cool when it shines.
I'd pull out his splinters
Without making him cry.
I'd always be there
If his dream was a nightmare.
My child.
My child.

There is a pause before MRS JOHNSTONE *nods.* MRS LYONS *goes across and kisses her, hugs her.* MRS JOHNSTONE *is slightly embarrassed.*

Oh. Now you must help me. There's so much . . . I'll have to . . . (*She takes out the cushion.*) We'll do this properly so that it's thoroughly convincing, and I'll need to see you walk, and baby clothes, I'll have to knit and buy bottles and suffer from piles.

MRS JOHNSTONE: What?

MRS LYONS: Doesn't one get piles when one's pregnant? And buy a cot and . . . Oh help me with this, Mrs J. Is it in the right place? (*She puts the cushion back again.*) I want it to look right before I go shopping.

MRS JOHNSTONE (*helping her with the false pregnancy*): What you goin' the shops for? I do the shopping.

MRS LYONS: Oh no, from now on I do the shopping. I want everyone to know about my baby. (*She suddenly reaches for the Bible.*)

Music.

Mrs J. We must make this a, erm, a binding agreement.

MRS LYONS *shows the Bible to* MRS JOHNSTONE, *who is at first reluctant and then lays her hand on it.*

The NARRATOR *enters. A bass note, repeated as a heartbeat.*

NARRATOR: In the name of Jesus, the thing was done,
Now there's no going back, for anyone.
It's too late now, for feeling torn
There's a pact been sealed, there's a deal been born.

MRS LYONS *puts the Bible away.* MRS JOHNSTONE *stands and stares as* MRS LYONS *grabs shopping bags and takes a last satisfied glance at herself in the mirror.*

MRS JOHNSTONE: Why . . . why did we have to do that?

MRS LYONS: Mrs J, nobody must ever know. Therefore we have to have an agreement.

MRS JOHNSTONE *nods but is still uncomfortable.*

Right, I shan't be long. Bye.

MRS LYONS *exits.*

MRS JOHNSTONE *stands alone, afraid.*

The heartbeat grows in intensity.

NARRATOR: How swiftly those who've made a pact,
Can come to overlook the fact.
Or wish the reckoning to be delayed
But a debt is a debt, and must be paid.

The NARRATOR *exits.*

As the heartbeat reaches maximum volume it suddenly stops and is replaced by the sound of crying babies.

Two nurses appear, each carrying a bundle. A pram is wheeled on.

The nurses hand the bundles to MRS JOHNSTONE *who places them smiling, into the pram. Making faces and noises at the babies she stops the crying. The babies settled, she sets off, wheeling the pram towards home.*

Various debt collectors emerge from her house to confront MRS JOHNSTONE.

CATALOGUE MAN: I'm sorry love . . . the kids said you were at the hospital. (*He looks into the pram.*) Ah . . . they're lovely, aren't they? I'm sorry love, especially at a time like this, but, you are twelve weeks behind in your payments. I've got to do this, girl . . .

FINANCE MAN: Y' shouldn't sign for the bloody stuff, missis. If y' know y' can't pay, y' shouldn't bloody well sign.

CATALOGUE MAN: Look, if y' could give me a couple of

weeks' money on this I could leave it.
MRS JOHNSTONE *shakes her head.*

FINANCE MAN: Y' shouldn't have signed for all this stuff, should y'? Y' knew y' wouldn't be able to pay, didn't y'?

MRS JOHNSTONE (*almost to herself*): When I got me job, I thought I would be able to pay. When I went in the showroom I only meant to come out with a couple of things. But when you're standing there, it all looks so nice. When y' look in the catalogue an' there's six months to pay, it seems years away, an' y' need a few things so y' sign.

FINANCE MAN: Yeh, well y' bloody well shouldn't.

MRS JOHNSTONE (*coming out of her trance; angrily*): I know I shouldn't, you soft get. I've spent all me bleedin' life knowin' I *shouldn't*. But I do. Now, take y' soddin' wireless and get off.

CATALOGUE MAN: Honest love, I'm sorry.

MRS JOHNSTONE: It's all right lad . . . we're used to it. We were in the middle of our tea one night when they arrived for the table. (*She gives a wry laugh.*)

CATALOGUE MAN: Ah well as long as y' can laugh about it, eh, that's the main thing isn't it?
The CATALOGUE MAN *exits.*

MRS JOHNSTONE (*not laughing*): Yeh.
Other creditors continue to enter the house and leave with goods.
MRS JOHNSTONE *watches the creditors. The babies begin to cry and she moves to the pram, rocking it gently as she sings, as if to the babies in the pram.* (*Singing*)

Only mine until
The time comes round
To pay the bill.
Then, I'm afraid,
What can't be paid
Must be returned.
You never, ever learn,
That nothing's yours,
On easy terms.
Only for a time,
I must not learn,
To call you mine.
Familiarize
That face, those eyes

Make future plans
That cannot be confirmed.
On borrowed time,
On easy terms.

Living on the never never,
Constant as the changing weather,
Never sure
Who's at the door
Or the price I'll have to pay.

Should we meet again
I will not recognize your name.
You can be sure
What's gone before
Will be concealed.
Your friends will never learn
That once we were
On easy terms.

Living on the never never,
Constant as the changing weather,
Never sure
Who's at the door
Or the price I'll have to pay . . .

MRS LYONS *enters, still with the pregnancy padding.*

MRS LYONS: They're born, you didn't notify me.

MRS JOHNSTONE: Well I . . . I just . . . it's . . . couldn't I keep them for a few more days, please, please, they're a pair, they go together.

MRS LYONS: My husband is due back tomorrow, Mrs Johnstone. I must have my baby. We made an agreement, a bargain. You swore on the Bible.

MRS JOHNSTONE: You'd better . . . you'd better see which one you want.

MRS LYONS: I'll take . . .

MRS JOHNSTONE: No. Don't tell me which one. Just take him, take him. (*Singing*)

Living on the never never,
Constant as the changing weather,
Never sure
Who's at the door
Or the price I'll have to pay,
Should we meet again . . .

MRS LYONS *rapidly pulls out the padding from beneath her dress. Amongst it is a shawl which she uses to wrap around the baby before picking it up from the pram.*

MRS LYONS: Thank you Mrs Johnstone, thank you. I'll see you next week.

MRS JOHNSTONE: I'm due back tomorrow.

MRS LYONS: I know but why don't you . . . why don't you take the week off, on full pay of course.

MRS LYON *exits.*

MRS JOHNSTONE *turns and enters her house with the remaining twin in the pram.*

KID ONE (*off*): What happened to the other twin, Mother?

KID TWO (*off*): Where's the other twinny, Mam?

MRS JOHNSTONE: He's gone. He's gone up to heaven, love. He's living with Jesus and the angels.

KID THREE (*off*): What's it like there Mam, in heaven?

MRS JOHNSTONE: It's lovely son, he'll be well looked after there. He'll have anything he wants.

KID ONE (*off*): Will he have his own bike?

MRS JOHNSTONE: Yeh. With both wheels on.

KID ONE (*off*): Why can't I have a bike? Eh?

MRS JOHNSTONE: I'll . . . I'll have a look in the catalogue next week. We'll see what the bikes are like in there.

KIDS (*together, off*): Mam, I want a Meccano set.
You said I could have a new dress, Mother.
Why can't I have an air pistol?
Let's look in the catalogue now, Mam.
It's great when we look in the catalogue, Mam.
Go on, let's all look in the catalogue.

MRS JOHNSTONE: I've told y', when I get home, I've got to go to work.

MR and MRS LYONS *enter their house and we see them looking at the child in its cot.*

MRS JOHNSTONE *enters and immediately goes about her work.*

MRS JOHNSTONE *stops work for a moment and glances into the cot, beaming and cooing.* MR LYONS *is next to her with* MRS LYONS *in the background, obviously agitated at* MRS JOHNSTON*'s fussing.*

Aw, he's really comin' on now, isn't he, Mr Lyons? I'll bet y' dead proud of him, aren't y', aren't y', eh?

MR LYONS (*good naturedly*): Yes . . . yes I am, aren't I Edward? I'm proud of Jennifer, too.

MR LYONS *beams at his wife who can hardly raise a smile.*

MRS JOHNSTONE: Ah . . . he's lovely. (*She coos into the cot.*) Ah look, he wants to be picked up, I'll just . . .

MRS LYONS: No, no, Mrs Johnstone. He's fine. He doesn't want to be picked up.

MRS JOHNSTONE: Ah, but look he's gonna cry . . .

MRS LYONS: If he needs picking up, *I* shall pick him up. All right?

MRS JOHNSTONE: Well, I just thought, I'm sorry I . . .

MRS LYONS: Yes. Erm, has the bathroom been done? Time is getting on.

MRS JOHNSTONE: Oh. Yeh, yeh . . .

MRS JOHNSTONE *exits.*

MR LYONS: Darling. Don't be hard on the woman. She only wanted to hold the baby. All women like to hold babies, don't they?

MRS LYONS: I don't want her to hold the baby, Richard. She's . . . I don't want the baby to catch anything. Babies catch things very easily, Richard.

MR LYONS: All right, all right, you know best.

MRS LYONS: You don't see her as much as I do. She's always fussing over him; any opportunity and she's cooing and cuddling as if she were his mother. She's always bothering him, Richard, always. Since the baby arrived she ignores most of her work. (*She is about to cry.*)

MR LYONS: Come on, come on . . . It's all right Jennifer. You're just a little . . . it's this depression thing that happens after a woman's had a . . .

MRS LYONS: I'm not depressed Richard; it's just that she makes me feel . . . Richard, I think she should go.

MR LYONS: And what will you do for help in the house?

MRS LYONS: I'll find somebody else. I'll find somebody who doesn't spend all day fussing over the baby.

MR LYONS (*glancing at his watch*): Oh well, I suppose you know best. The house is your domain. Look, Jen, I've got a board meeting. I really must dash.

MRS LYONS: Richard, can you let me have some cash?

MR LYONS: Of course.

MRS LYONS: I need about fifty pounds.

MR LYONS: My God, what for?

MRS LYONS: I've got lots of things to buy for the baby, I've got the nursery to sort out . . .

MR LYONS: All right, all right, here. (*He hands her the money.*)

MR LYONS *exits.*

MRS LYONS *considers what she is about to do and then calls*

MRS LYONS: Mrs Johnstone. Mrs Johnstone, would you come out here for a moment, please.

MRS JOHNSTONE *enters.*

MRS JOHNSTONE: Yes?

MRS LYONS. Sit down. Richard and I have been talking it over and, well the thing is, we both think it would be better if you left.

MRS JOHNSTONE: Left where?

MRS LYONS: It's your work. Your work has deteriorated.

MRS JOHNSTONE: But, I work the way I've always worked.

MRS LYONS: Well, I'm sorry, we're not satisfied.

MRS JOHNSTONE: What will I do? How are we gonna live without my job?

MRS LYONS: Yes, well we've thought of that. Here, here's . . . (*She pushes the money into* MRS JOHNSTONE*'s hands.*) It's a lot of money . . . but, well . . .

MRS JOHNSTONE (*thinking, desperate. Trying to get it together.*) OK. All right. All right, Mrs Lyons, right. If I'm goin', I'm takin' my son with me, I'm takin' . . .

As MRS JOHNSTONE *moves towards the cot* MRS LYONS *roughly drags her out of the way.*

MRS LYONS: Oh no, you're not. Edward is my son. Mine.

MRS JOHNSTONE: I'll tell someone . . . I'll tell the police . . . I'll bring the police in an' . . .

MRS LYONS: No . . . no you won't. You gave your baby away. Don't you realize what a crime that is. You'll be locked up. You sold your baby.

MRS JOHNSTONE, *horrified, sees the bundle of notes in her hand, and throws it across the room.*

MRS JOHNSTONE: I didn't . . . you told me, you said I could see him every day. Well, I'll tell someone, I'm gonna tell . . .

MRS JOHNSTONE *starts to leave but* MRS LYONS *stops her.*

MRS LYONS: No. You'll tell nobody.

Music.

Because . . . because if you tell anyone . . . and these children learn of the truth, then you know what will happen, don't you? You do know what they say about twins, secretly parted, don't you?

MRS JOHNSTONE (*terrified*): What? What?

MRS LYONS: They say . . . they say that if either twin learns that he once was a pair, they shall both immediately die. It means, Mrs Johnstone, that these brothers shall grow up, unaware of the other's existence. They shall be raised apart and never, ever told what was once the truth. You won't tell anyone about this, Mrs Johnstone, because if you do, you will kill them.

MRS LYONS *picks up the money and thrusts it into* MRS JOHNSTONE*'s hands.* MRS LYONS *turns and walks away.*

The NARRATOR *enters*

NARRATOR (*singing*): Shoes upon the table
An' a spider's been killed.
Someone broke the lookin' glass
A full moon shinin'
An' the salt's been spilled.
You're walkin' on the pavement cracks
Don't know what's gonna come to pass.

Now y' know the devil's got your number,
Y' know he's gonna find y',
Y' know he's right behind y',
He's starin' through your windows
He's creepin' down the hall.

Ain't no point in clutching
At your rosary
You're always gonna know what was done
Even when you shut your eyes you still see
That you sold a son
And you can't tell anyone.

But y' know the devil's got your number,
Y' know he's gonna find y',
Y' know he's right behind y',
He's starin' through your windows
He's creeping down the hall

Yes, y' know the devil's got your number
He's gonna find y',

Y' know he's right behind y',
He's standin' on your step
And he's knocking at your door.
He's knocking at your door,
He's knocking at your door.

The NARRATOR *exits.*

During the song MRS JOHNSTONE *has gone to her house and locked herself in.*

MICKEY, *aged 'seven' is knocking incessantly at the door. He is carrying a toy gun.*

MRS JOHNSTONE (*screaming; off*): Go away!

MICKEY: Mother . . . will y' open the bleedin' door or what?

MRS JOHNSTONE (*realizing; with relief; off*): Mickey?

MRS JOHNSTONE *comes to open the door.*

MICKEY: Mam, Mam.

She grabs him and hugs him. He extricates himself.

Why was the door bolted? Did you think it was the rent man?

She laughs and looks at him.

Mam, our Sammy's robbed me other gun an' that was me best one. Why does he rob all me things off me?

MRS JOHNSTONE: Because you're the youngest Mickey. It used to happen to our Sammy when he was the youngest.

MICKEY: Mam, we're playin' mounted police an' Indians. I'm a mountie. Mam, Mam, y' know this mornin', we've wiped out three thousand Indians.

MRS JOHNSTONE: Good.

MICKEY (*aiming the gun at her and firing*): Mam, Mam, you're dead.

MRS JOHNSTONE (*staring at him*): Hmm.

MICKEY: What's up, Mam?

MRS JOHNSTONE: Nothin' son. Go on, you go out an' play, there's a good lad. But, ey, don't you go playin' with those hooligans down at the rough end.

MICKEY (*on his way out*): We're down at the other end, near the big houses in the park.

MRS JOHNSTONE: Mickey! Come here.

MICKEY: What?

MRS JOHNSTONE: What did you say, where have you been playin'?

MICKEY: Mam, I'm sorry, I forgot.

MRS JOHNSTONE: What have I told you about playin' up near there. Come here. (*She grabs him.*)

MICKEY: It wasn't my fault. Honest.

MRS JOHNSTONE: So whose fault was it then?

MICKEY: The Indians. They rode up that way, they were tryin' to escape.

MRS JOHNSTONE: Don't you ever go up there. Do you hear me?

MICKEY: Yeh. You let our Sammy go up there.

MRS JOHNSTONE: Our Sammy's older than you.

MICKEY: But why . . .

MRS JOHNSTONE: Just shut up. Never mind why. You don't go up near there. Now go on, get out an' play. But you stay outside the front door where I can see y'.

MICKEY: Ah but, Mam, the . . .

MRS JOHNSTONE: Go on!

MRS JOHNSTONE *exits.*

MICKEY *makes his way outside. He is fed up. Desultory. Shoots down a few imaginary Indians but somehow the magic has gone out of genocide.*

MICKEY *sits, bored, looking at the ants on the pavement.*

MICKEY (*reciting*): I wish I was our Sammy
Our Sammy's nearly ten.
He's got two worms and a catapult
An' he's built a underground den.
But I'm not allowed to go in there,
I have to stay near the gate,
'Cos me Mam says I'm only seven,
But I'm not, I'm nearly eight!

I sometimes hate our Sammy,
He robbed me toy car y' know,
Now the wheels are missin' an' the top's broke off,
An' the bleedin' thing won't go.
An' he said when he took it, it was just like that,
But it wasn't, it went dead straight,
But y' can't say nott'n when they think y' seven
An' y' not, y' nearly eight.

I wish I was our Sammy,
Y' wanna see him spit,
Straight in y' eye from twenty yards
An' every time a hit.
He's allowed to play with matches,

And he goes to bed dead late,
And I have to go at seven,
Even though I'm nearly eight.

Y' know our Sammy,
He draws nudey women,
Without arms, or legs, or even heads
In the baths, when he goes swimmin'.
But I'm not allowed to go to the baths,
Me Mam says I have to wait,
'Cos I might get drowned, 'cos I'm only seven,
But I'm not, I'm nearly eight.

Y' know our Sammy,
Y' know what he sometimes does?
He wees straight through the letter box
Of the house next door to us.
I tried to do it one night,
But I had to stand on a crate,
'Cos I couldn't reach the letter box
But I will by the time I'm eight.

Bored and petulant, MICKEY *sits and shoots an imaginary Sammy.*

EDWARD, *also aged 'seven' appears. He is bright and forthcoming.*

EDWARD: Hello.

MICKEY (*suspiciously*): Hello.

EDWARD: I've seen you before.

MICKEY: Where?

EDWARD: You were playing with some other boys near my house.

MICKEY: Do you live up in the park?

EDWARD: Yes. Are you going to come and play up there again?

MICKEY: No. I would do but I'm not allowed.

EDWARD: Why?

MICKEY: 'Cos me mam says.

EDWARD: Well, my mummy doesn't allow me to play down here actually.

MICKEY: 'Gis a sweet.

EDWARD: All right. (*He offers a bag from his pocket.*)

MICKEY (*shocked*): What?

EDWARD: Here.

MICKEY (*trying to work out the catch. Suspiciously taking one*): Can I have another one. For our Sammy?

EDWARD: Yes, of course. Take as many as you want.

MICKEY (*taking a handful*): Are you soft?

EDWARD: I don't think so.

MICKEY: Round here if y' ask for a sweet, y' have to ask about, about twenty million times. An' y' know what?

EDWARD (*sitting beside* MICKEY): What?

MICKEY: They still don't bleedin' give y' one. Sometimes our Sammy does but y' have to be dead careful if our Sammy gives y' a sweet.

EDWARD: Why?

MICKEY: 'Cos, if our Sammy gives y' a sweet he's usually weed on it first.

EDWARD (*exploding in giggles*): Oh, that sounds like super fun.

MICKEY: It is. If y' our Sammy.

EDWARD: Do you want to come and play?

MICKEY: I might do. But I'm not playin' now 'cos I'm pissed off.

EDWARD (*awed*): Pissed off. You say smashing things don't you? Do you know any more words like that?

MICKEY: Yeh. Yeh, I know loads of words like that. Y' know, like the 'F' word.

EDWARD (*clueless*): Pardon?

MICKEY: The 'F' word.

EDWARD *is still puzzled.* MICKEY *looks round to check that he cannot be overheard, then whispers the word to* EDWARD. *The two of them immediately wriggle and giggle with glee.*

EDWARD: What does it mean?

MICKEY: I don't know. It sounds good though, doesn't it?

EDWARD: Fantastic. When I get home I'll look it up in the dictionary.

MICKEY: In the what?

EDWARD: The dictionary. Don't you know what a dictionary is?

MICKEY: 'Course I do. . . . It's a, it's a thingy innit?

EDWARD: A book which explains the meaning of words.

MICKEY: The meaning of words, yeh. Our Sammy'll be here soon. I hope he's in a good mood. He's dead mean sometimes.

EDWARD: Why?

MICKEY: It's 'cos he's got a plate in his head.

EDWARD: A plate. In his head?

MICKEY: Yeh. When he was little, me Mam was at work an' our Donna Marie was supposed to be lookin' after him but he fell out the window an' broke his head. So they took him to the hospital an' put a plate in his head.

EDWARD: A plate. A dinner plate?

MICKEY: I don't think so, 'cos our Sammy's head's not really that big. I think it must have been one of them little plates that you have bread off.

EDWARD: A side plate?

MICKEY: No, it's on the top.

EDWARD: And . . . and can you see the shape of it, in his head?

MICKEY: I suppose, I suppose if y' looked under his hair.

EDWARD (*after a reflective pause*): You know the most smashing things. Will you be my best friend?

MICKEY: Yeh. If y' want.

EDWARD: What's your name?

MICKEY: Michael Johnstone. But everyone calls me Mickey. What's yours?

EDWARD: Edward Lyons.

MICKEY: D' they call y' Eddie?

EDWARD: No.

MICKEY: Well, I will.

EDWARD: Will you?

MICKEY: Yeh. How old are y' Eddie?

EDWARD: Seven.

MICKEY: I'm older than you. I'm nearly eight.

EDWARD: Well, I'm nearly eight, really.

MICKEY: What's your birthday?

EDWARD: July the eighteenth.

MICKEY: So is mine.

EDWARD: Is it really?

MICKEY: Ey, we were born on the same day . . . that means we can be blood brothers. Do you wanna be my blood brother, Eddie?

EDWARD: Yes, please.

MICKEY (*producing a penknife*): It hurts y' know. (*He puts a nick in his hand.*) Now, give us yours.

MICKEY *nicks* EDWARD*'s hand, then they clamp hands together.*

See this means that we're blood brothers, an' that we always have to stand by each other. Now you say after me: 'I will always defend my brother'.

EDWARD: I will always defend my brother . . .

MICKEY: And stand by him.

EDWARD: And stand by him.

MICKEY: An' share all my sweets with him.

EDWARD: And share . . .

SAMMY *leaps in front of them, gun in hand, pointed at them.*

MICKEY: Hi ya, Sammy.

SAMMY: Give us a sweet.

MICKEY: Haven't got any.

EDWARD: Yes, you have . . .

MICKEY *frantically shakes his head, trying to shut* EDWARD *up.*

Yes, I gave you one for Sammy, remember?

SAMMY *laughs at* EDWARD*'s voice and* MICKEY*'s misfortune.*

SAMMY: Y' little robbin' get.

MICKEY: No, I'm not. (*He hands over a sweet.*) An' anyway, you pinched my best gun.

MICKEY *tries to snatch the gun from* SAMMY, *but* SAMMY *is too fast.*

SAMMY: It's last anyway. It only fires caps. I'm gonna get a real gun soon, I'm gonna get an air gun.

SAMMY *goes into a fantasy shoot out. He doesn't notice* EDWARD *who has approached him and is craning to get a close look at his head.*

(*Eventually noticing*) What are you lookin' at?

EDWARD: Pardon.

MICKEY: That's Eddie. He lives up by the park.

SAMMY: He's a friggin' poshy.

MICKEY: No, he's not. He's my best friend.

SAMMY (*snorting, deciding it's not worth the bother*): You're soft. Y' just soft little kids. (*In quiet disdain he moves away.*)

MICKEY: Where y' goin'?

SAMMY (*looking at* MICKEY): I'm gonna do another burial. Me worms have died again.

MICKEY (*excitedly; to* EDWARD): Oh, y' comin' the funeral? Our Sammy is having a funeral. Can we come, Sammy?

SAMMY *puts his hand into his pocket and brings forth a handful of soil.*

SAMMY: Look, they was alive an wrigglin' this mornin'. But by dinner time they was dead.

MICKEY *and* EDWARD *inspect the deceased worms in* SAMMY*'s hand.*

MRS JOHNSTONE *enters.*

MRS JOHNSTONE: Mickey . . . Mickey . . .

EDWARD: Is that your mummy?

MICKEY: Mam . . . Mam, this is my brother.

MRS JOHNSTONE (*stunned*): What?

MICKEY: My blood brother, Eddie.

MRS JOHNSTONE: Eddie, Eddie who?

EDWARD: Edward Lyons, Mrs Johnstone.

MRS JOHNSTONE *stands still, staring at him.*

MICKEY: Eddie's my best friend, Mam. He lives up by the park an' . . .

MRS JOHNSTONE: Mickey . . . get in the house.

MICKEY: What?

MRS JOHNSTONE: Sammy, you an' all. Both of y' get in.

SAMMY: But I'm older than him, I don't have to . . .

MRS JOHNSTONE: I said get, the pair of y' . . .

MICKEY (*going, almost in tears*): But I haven't done nothin'. I'll see y' Eddie. Ta ra, Eddie . . .

MICKEY *exits.*

MRS JOHNSTONE: Sammy!

SAMMY: Ah. (*To* EDWARD.) I'll get you.

EDWARD: Have I done something wrong, Mrs Johnstone?

MRS JOHNSTONE: Does your mother know that you're down here?

EDWARD *shakes his head.*

An' what would she say if she did know?

EDWARD: I . . . I think she's be angry?

MRS JOHNSTONE: So don't you think you better get home before she finds out?

EDWARD: Yes.

MRS JOHNSTONE: Go on, then.

EDWARD *turns to go, then stops.*

EDWARD: Could I . . . would it be all right if I came to play with Mickey on another day? Or perhaps he could come to play at my house . . .

MRS JOHNSTONE: Don't you ever come round here again. Ever.

EDWARD: But . . .

MRS JOHNSTONE: Ever! Now go on. Beat it, go home before the bogey man gets y'.

EDWARD *walks towards his home. As he goes* MRS JOHNSTONE *sings*

Should we meet again,
I will not recognize your name,
You can be sure
What's gone before
Will be concealed.
Your friends will never learn
That once we were
On easy terms.

MR and MRS LYONS *enter their house as* EDWARD *walks home.*

EDWARD *reaches his home and walks in. His mother hugs him and his father produces a toy gun for him.* EDWARD, *delighted, seizes it and 'shoots' his father, who spiritedly 'dies' to* EDWARD*'s great amusement.* EDWARD *and his father romp on the floor.* MRS LYONS *settles herself in an armchair with a story book, calling* EDWARD *over to her.* EDWARD *goes and sits with her,* MR LYONS *joining them and sitting on the arm of the chair.*

MRS JOHNSTONE *turns and goes into her house at the end of the song.*

MR LYONS *gets up and walks towards the door.*

EDWARD: Daddy . . . we haven't finished the story yet.

MR LYONS: Mummy will read the story, Edward. I've got to go to work for an hour.

MRS LYONS *gets up and goes to her husband,* EDWARD *goes to the bookshelf and leafs through a dictionary.*

MRS LYONS: Richard you didn't say . . .

MR LYONS: Darling, I'm sorry, but if, if we complete this merger I will, I promise you, have more time. That's why we're doing it, Jen. If we complete this, the firm will run itself and I'll have plenty of time to spend with you both.

MRS LYONS: I just – it's not me, it's Edward. You should spend more time with him. I don't want – I don't want him growing away from you.

EDWARD: Daddy, how do you spell bogey man?

MR LYONS: Ask Mummy. Darling, I'll see you later now. Must dash.

MR LYONS *exits.*

EDWARD: Mummy, how do you spell bogey man?

MRS LYONS: Mm?

EDWARD: Bogey man?

MRS LYONS (*laughing*): Edward, whever did you hear such a thing?

EDWARD: I'm trying to look it up.

MRS LYONS: There's no such thing as a bogey man. It's a – a superstition. The sort of thing a silly mother might say to her children – 'the bogey man will get you'.

EDWARD: Will he get me?

MRS LYONS: Edward, I've told you, there's no such thing.

A doorbell is heard.

MRS LYONS *goes to answer the door.*

MICKEY (*off*): Does Eddie live here?

MRS LYONS (*off*): Pardon?

MICKEY (*off*): Does he? Is he comin' out to play, eh?

EDWARD (*shouting*): Mickey!

MICKEY *enters, pursued by* MRS LYONS.

MICKEY: Hi-ya, Eddie. I've got our Sammy's catapult. Y' comin' out?

EDWARD: Oh! (*He takes the catapult and trys a practice shot.*) Isn't Mickey fantastic, Mum?

MRS LYONS: Do you go to the same school as Edward?

MICKEY: No.

EDWARD: Mickey says smashing things. We're blood brothers, aren't we, Mickey?

MICKEY: Yeh. We were born on the same day.

EDWARD: Come on Mickey, let's go . . .

MRS LYONS: Edward . . . Edward, it's time for bed.

EDWARD: Mummy. It's not.

MRS LYONS *takes over and ushers* MICKEY *out.*

MRS LYONS: I'm very sorry, but it's Edward's bedtime.

EDWARD: Mummy. Mummy, it's early.

MRS LYONS *exits with* MICKEY *to show him out. Then she returns.*

Mummy!

MRS LYONS: Edward. Edward where did you meet that boy?

EDWARD: At his house.

MRS LYONS: And . . . and his second name is Johnstone, isn't it?

EDWARD: Yes. And I think you're very, very mean.

MRS LYONS: I've told you never to go where that boy – where boys like that live.

EDWARD: But why?

MRS LYONS: Because, because you're not the same as him. You're not, do you understand?

EDWARD: No, I don't understand. And I hate you!

MRS LYONS (*almost crying*): Edward, Edward, don't. It's . . . what I'm doing is only for your own good. It's only because I love you, Edward.

EDWARD: You don't you don't. If you loved me you'd let me go out with Mickey because he's my best friend. I like him more than you.

MRS LYONS: Edward. Edward don't say that. Don't ever say that.

EDWARD: Well. Well it's true. And I will say it. I know what you are.

MRS LYONS: What? What!

EDWARD: You're . . . you're a fuckoff!

MRS LYONS *hits* EDWARD *hard and instinctively.*

MRS LYONS: You see, you see why I don't want you mixing with boys like that! You learn filth from them and behave like this like a, like a horrible little boy, like them. But you are not like them. You are my son, mine, and you won't, you won't ever . . .

She notices the terror in EDWARD*'s face and realizes how heavy she has been. Gently she pulls him to her and cradles him.*

Oh, my son . . . my beautiful, beautiful son.

The scene fades as the next scene begins. We hear cap guns and the sound of children making Indian whoops.

The children rush on into the street playing cowboys and Indians; cops and robbers; goodies and baddies etc.

During the battle MRS LYONS *exits.*

EDWARD *remains on stage, in the background, as though in his garden, watching, unnoticed by the battling children.*

MICKEY *and* LINDA *are in one gang,* SAMMY *in another.*

SAMMY (*singing acapella, kids' rhyme*):
I got y'
I shot y'
An' y' bloody know I did
I got y'
I shot y'

LINDA: I stopped it with the bin lid.

There is a mass of derisive jeers from the other side.

Music.

(*Singing*): But you know that if you cross your fingers
And if you count from one to ten
You can get up off the ground again
It doesn't matter
The whole thing's just a game.

The shooting starts all over again. A KID *raps on the door of a house.* LINDA, *as a 'Moll' appears.*

KID: My name is Elliot Ness,
And lady, here's my card,
I'm lookin' for one Al Capone

(*To* LACKEYS):
Mac, check the back
Sarge, you check the yard!

LINDA: But pal, I've told y'
Al ain't home.

We see 'Al' make a break for it. NESS *shoots him like he was eating his breakfast.*

KID: So, lady can I use your telephone.

As NESS *goes to the phone and orders a hearse we see* AL *get up and sing the chorus with the other children*

But you know that if you cross your fingers,
And if you count from one to ten,
You can get up off the ground again,
It doesn't matter the whole thing's just a game.

The KID *who was playing* AL *becomes a cowboy. He turns to face* SAMMY *and sings*

COWBOY: When I say draw,
You'd better grab that gun,
An' maybe say a little prayer

Cos I'm the fastest draw
That man you ever saw.
Call up your woman, say goodbye to her,
Cos y' know you're goin' right down there.

As he draws his gun on SAMMY, SAMMY *produces a bazooka and blows him off the stage.*

ALL: But you know that if you cross your fingers,
And if you count from one to ten,
You can get up off the ground again,
It doesn't matter,
The whole thing's just a game.

A small group of CHILDREN *become a brigade of US troops.*

SERGEANT: OK men, let's get them
With a hand grenade.

CORPORAL: Let's see them try and get outta this.

REST: He's a hot shot Sergeant
From the Ninth Brigade
He's never been known to miss

SERGEANT (*to grenade*): C'mon give Daddy a kiss. (*He pulls the pin and lobs it.*)

His BRIGADE *cover their ears and crouch down.* LINDA *catches the grenade and lobs it back at them. After being blown to pieces they get up singing the chorus, along with the 'enemy'.*

ALL: But you know that if you cross your fingers,
And if you count from one to ten.
You can get up off the ground again,
It doesn't matter,
The whole thing's just a game.

SAMMY *comes forward as* PROFESSOR HOWE *carrying a condom filled with water.*

PROFESSOR: My name's Professor Howe,
An' zees bomb I 'old,
Eet can destroy ze 'emisphere,
I've primed it, I've timed it
To explode,
Unless you let me out of here (NO?)

They don't.

Then I suggest you cover your ears.

There is an explosion which tops them all. Out of it come all the children singing the chorus.

ALL: But you know that if you cross your fingers,
And if you count from one to ten,
you can get up off the ground again,
It doesn't matter,
The whole thing's just a game
The whole thing's just a game
The whole thing's just a . . .

SAMMY (*interrupting; chanting*):
You're dead
Y' know y' are
I got y' standin'
Near that car.

LINDA: But when y' did
His hand was hid
Behind his back
His fingers crossed
An' so he's not

MICKEY: So you fuck off!

All the children, apart from MICKEY *and* LINDA, *point and chant the accusing 'Aah!'* MICKEY *is singled out, accused. The rest, led by* SAMMY *suddenly chant at* MICKEY *and point*

ALL (*chanting*): You said the 'F' word
You're gonna die
You'll go to hell an' there you'll fry
Just like a fish in a chip shop fat
Only twenty five million times hotter than that!

They all laugh at MICKEY.

LINDA *moves in to protect* MICKEY *who is visibly shaken.*

LINDA: Well, well, all youse lot swear, so you'll all go to hell with him.

SAMMY: No, we won't Linda.

LINDA: Why?

SAMMY: 'Cos when we swear . . . we cross our fingers!

MICKEY: Well, my fingers were crossed.

CHILDREN (*variously*): No they were't.
Liar!
Come off it.
I seen them.

LINDA: Leave him alone!

SAMMY: Why? What'll you do about it if we don't?

LINDA (*undaunted; approaching* SAMMY): I'll tell my mother

why all her ciggies always disappear when you're in our house.

SAMMY: What?

LINDA: An' the half crowns.

SAMMY (*suddenly*): Come on gang, let's go. We don't wanna play with these anyway. They're just kids.

The other children fire a barrage of 'shots' at MICKEY *and* LINDA *before they rush off.*

LINDA: I hate them!

LINDA *notices* MICKEY *quietly crying.*

What's up?

MICKY: I don't wanna die.

LINDA: But y' have to Mickey. Everyone does. (*She starts to dry his tears.*) Like your twinny died, didn't he, when he was a baby. See, look on the bright side of it, Mickey. When you die you'll meet your twinny again, won't y'?

MICKEY: Yeh.

LINDA: An' listen Mickey, if y' dead, there's no school, is there?

MICKEY (*smiling*): An' I don't care about our Sammy, anyway. Look. (*He produces an air pistol.*) He thinks no one knows he's got it. But I know where he hides it.

LINDA (*impressed*): Ooh . . . gis a go.

MICKEY: No . . . come on, let's go get Eddie first.

LINDA: Who?

MICKEY: Come on, I'll show y'.

They go as if to EDWARD*'s garden.*

MICKEY (*loud but conspiratorially*): Eddie . . . Eddie . . . y' comin' out?

EDWARD: I . . . My mum says I haven't got to play with you.

MICKEY: Well, my mum says I haven't got to play with you. But take no notice of mothers. They're soft. Come on, I've got Linda with me. She's a girl but she's all right.

EDWARD *decides to risk it and creeps out.*

MICKEY: Hi-ya.

EDWARD: Hi-ya, Mickey. Hello, Linda.

LINDA: Hi-ya, Eddie. (*She produces the air pistol.*) Look . . . we've got Sammy's air gun.

MICKEY: Come on, Eddie. You can have a shot at our target in the park.

LINDA: Peter Pan.

MICKEY: We always shoot at that, don't we Linda?

LINDA: Yeh, we try an' shoot his little thingy off, don't we, Mickey?

They all laugh.

Come on gang, let's go.

EDWARD (*standing firm*): But Mickey . . . I mean . . . suppose we get caught . . . by a policeman.

MICKEY: Aah . . . take no notice. We've been caught loads of times by a policeman . . . haven't we, Linda?

LINDA: Oh, my God, yeh. Hundreds of times. More than that.

MICKEY: We say dead funny things to them, don't we, Linda?

EDWARD: What sort of funny things?

LINDA: All sorts, don't we Mickey?

MICKEY: Yeh . . . like y' know when they ask what y' name is, we say things like, like 'Adolph Hitler', don't we Linda?

LINDA: Yeh, an' hey Eddie, y' know when they say, 'What d' y' think you're doin'?' we always say somethin' like like, 'waitin' for the ninety-two bus'.

MICKEY *and* LINDA *crease up with laughter.*

Come on.

EDWARD (*greatly impressed*): Do you . . . do you really? Goodness, that's fantastic.

MICKEY: Come on, bunk under y' fence, y' Ma won't see y'.

MICKEY, LINDA *and* EDWARD *exit.*

MRS LYONS *enters the garden.*

MRS LYONS (*calling*): Edward, Edward, Edward . . .

The NARRATOR *enters.*

Music.

NARRATOR (*singing*): There's gypsies in the wood,
An' they've been watchin' you,
They're gonna take your baby away.
There's gypsies in the wood,
An' they've been calling you,
Can Edward please come out and play,
Please can he come with us and play.

You know the devil's got your number,
Y' know he's gonna find y',
Y' know he's right behind y',
He's staring through your windows,
He's creeping down the hall.

MR LYONS *enters the garden.*

MRS LYONS: Oh Richard, Richard.

MR LYONS: For God's sake Jennifer, I told you on the phone, he'll just be out playing somewhere.

MRS LYONS: But where?

MR LYONS: Outside somewhere, with friends. Edward . . .

MRS LYONS: But I don't want him out playing.

MR LYONS: Jennifer, he's not a baby. Edward . . .

MRS LYONS: I don't care, I don't care . . .

MR LYONS: For Christ's sake, you bring me home from work in the middle of the day, just to say you haven't seen him for an hour. Perhaps we should be talking about you getting something for your nerves.

MRS LYONS: There's nothing wrong with my nerves. It's just . . . just this place . . . I hate it. Richard, I don't want to stay here any more. I want to move.

MR LYONS: Jennifer! Jennifer, how many times . . . the factory is here, my work is here . . .

MRS LYONS: It doesn't have to be somewhere far away. But we have got to move, Richard. Because if we stay here I feel that something terrible will happen, something bad.

MR LYONS *sighs and puts his arm round* MRS LYONS.

MR LYONS: Look, Jen. What is this thing you keep talking about getting away from? Mm?

MRS LYONS: It's just . . . it's these people . . . these people that Edward has started mixing with. Can't you see how he's drawn to them? They're . . . they're drawing him away from me.

MR LYONS, *in despair, turns away from her.*

MR LYONS. Oh Christ.

He turns to look at her but she looks away. He sighs and absently bends to pick up a pair of children's shoes from the floor.

I really do think you should see a doctor.

MRS LYONS (*snapping*): I don't need to see a doctor. I just need to move away from this neighbourhood, because I'm frightened. I'm frightened for Edward.

MR LYONS *places the shoes on the table before turning on her.*

MR LYONS: Frightened of what, woman?

MRS LYONS (*wheeling to face him*): Frightened of . . . (*She is stopped by the sight of the shoes on the table. She rushes at the table and sweeps the shoes off.*)

Music.

NARRATOR (*singing*): There's shoes upon the table
An' a spider's been killed
Someone broke the lookin' glass
There's a full moon shinin'
An' the salt's been spilled
You're walkin' on pavement cracks
Don't know what's gonna come to pass
Now you know the devil's got your number
He's gonna find y'
Y' know he's right beyind y'
He's starin' through your windows
He's creeping down the hall.

The song ends with a percussion build to a sudden full stop and the scene snaps from MRS LYONS *to the children.*

MICKEY, EDDIE *and* LINDA *are standing in line, taking it in turns to fire the air pistol.* MICKEY *takes aim and fires.*

LINDA (*with glee*): Missed.

EDWARD *loads and fires.*

Missed!

LINDA *takes the gun and fires. We hear a metallic ping. She beams a satisfied smile at* MICKEY *who ignores it and reloads, fires. The routine is repeated with exactly the same outcome until*

MICKEY (*taking the gun*): We're not playin' with the gun no more. (*He puts it away.*)

LINDA: Ah, why?

MICKEY: It gets broke if y' use it too much.

EDWARD: What are we going to do now, Mickey?

MICKEY: I dunno.

LINDA: I do.

MICKEY: What?

LINDA: Let's throw some stones through them windows.

MICKEY (*brightening*): Ooh, I dare y' Linda, I dare y'.

LINDA (*bending for a stone*): Well, I will. I'm not scared, either. Are you Eddie?

EDWARD: Erm . . . well . . . erm . . .

LINDA: He is look. Eddie's scared.

MICKEY: No, he isn't! Are y', Eddie?

EDWARD (*stoically*): No . . . I'm not. I'm not scared at all, actually.

LINDA: Right, when I count to three we all throw together. One, two, three . . .

Unseen by them a POLICEMAN *has approached behind them.*

POLICEMAN: Me mother caught a flea, she put it in the tea pot to make a cup of tea . . . And what do you think you're doing?

LINDA *and* MICKEY *shoot terrified glances at* EDWARD, *almost wetting themselves.*

EDWARD (*mistaking their look for encouragement*): Waiting for the ninety-two bus. (*He explodes with excited laughter.*)

LINDA: He's not with us.

MICKEY: Sir.

LINDA: Sir.

POLICEMAN: No. He's definitely with us. What's your name, son?

EDWARD: Adolph Hitler.

EDWARD *laughs until through the laughter he senses that all is not well. He sees that he alone is laughing. The laughter turns to tears which sets the other two off.*

The three children turn round, crying, bawling, followed by the POLICEMAN.

The three children exit.

MRS JOHNSTONE *enters.*

The POLICEMAN *goes to confront* MRS JOHNSTONE.

POLICEMAN: And he was about to commit a serious crime, love. Now, do you understand that? You don't wanna end up in court again, do y'?

MRS JOHNSTONE *shakes her head.*

Well, that's what's gonna happen if I have any more trouble from one of yours. I warned you last time, didn't I, Mrs Johnstone, about your Sammy?

MRS JOHNSTONE *nods.*

Well, there'll be no more bloody warnings from now on. Either you keep them in order, Missis, or it'll be the courts for you, or worse, won't it?

MRS JOHNSTONE *nods.*

Yes, it will.

As the POLICEMAN *turns and goes towards the* LYON*'s house music is heard.*

MRS JOHNSTONE (*singing*): Maybe some day
We'll move away
And start all over again
In some new place

Where they don't know my face
And nobody's heard of my name
Where we can begin again
Feel we can win an' then . . .
Maybe . . .

The music tails off as we see the POLICEMAN *confronting* MR LYONS. *The* POLICEMAN *has removed his helmet and holds a glass of scotch.* EDWARD *is there.*

POLICEMAN: An' er, as I say, it was more of a prank, really, Mr Lyons. I'd just dock his pocket money if I was you. (*Laughs.*) But, one thing I would say, if y' don't mind me sayin', is well, I'm not sure I'd let him mix with the likes of them in the future. Make sure he keeps with his own kind, Mr Lyons. Well, er, thanks for the drink, sir. All the best now. He's a good lad, aren't you Adolph? Goodnight, sir. (*He replaces his helmet.*)

The POLICEMAN *leaves.*

MR LYONS: Edward . . . how would you like to move to another house?

EDWARD: Why, Daddy?

MR LYONS: Erm, well, various reasons really. Erm, actually Mummy's not been too well lately and we thought a move, perhaps further out towards the country somewhere, might . . . Do you think you'd like that?

EDWARD: I want to stay here.

MR LYONS: Well, you think about it, old chap.

EDWARD *leaves his home and goes to the* JOHNSTONE*'s door. He knocks at the door.*

MRS JOHNSTONE *answers the door.*

EDWARD: Hello, Mrs Johnstone. How are you?

MRS JOHNSTONE: You what?

EDWARD: I'm sorry. Is there something wrong?

MRS JOHNSTONE: No, I just . . . I don't usually have kids enquiring about my health. I'm er . . . I'm all right. An' how are you, Master Lyons?

EDWARD: Very well, thank you.

MRS JOHNSTONE *looks at* EDWARD *for a moment.*

MRS JOHNSTONE: Yeh. You look it. Y' look very well. Does your mother look after you?

EDWARD: Of course.

MRS JOHNSTONE: Now listen, Eddie, I told you not to come around here again.

EDWARD: I'm sorry but I just wanted to see Mickey.

MRS JOHNSTONE: No. It's best . . . if . . .

EDWARD: I won't be coming here again. Ever. We're moving away. To the country.

MRS JOHNSTONE: Lucky you.

EDWARD: But I'd much rather live here.

MRS JOHNSTONE: Would you? When are y' goin'?

EDWARD: Tomorrow.

MRS JOHNSTONE: Oh. So we really won't see you again, eh . . .
EDWARD *shakes his head and begins to cry.*
What's up?

EDWARD (*through his tears*): I don't want to go. I want to stay here where my friends are . . . where Mickey is.

MRS JOHNSTONE: Come here.
She takes him, cradling him, letting him cry.
No listen . . . listen, don't you be soft. You'll probably love it in your new house. You'll meet lots of new friends an' in no time at all you'll forget Mickey ever existed.

EDWARD: I won't . . . I won't. I'll never forget.

MRS JOHNSTONE: Shush, shush. Listen, listen Eddie, here's you wantin' to stay here, an' here's me, I've been tryin' to get out for years. We're a right pair, aren't we, you an' me?

EDWARD: Why don't you Mrs Johnstone? Why don't you buy a new house near us?

MRS JOHNSTONE: Just like that?

EDWARD: Yes, yes.

MRS JOHNSTONE: Ey.

EDWARD: Yes.

MRS JOHNSTONE: Would you like a picture of Mickey, to take with you? So's you could remember him?

EDWARD: Yes, please.
She removes a locket from around her neck.

MRS JOHNSTONE: See, look . . . there's Mickey, there. He was just a young kid when that was taken.

EDWARD: And is that you Mrs Johnstone?
She nods:
Can I really have this?

MRS JOHNSTONE: Yeh. But keep it a secret eh, Eddie? Just our secret, between you an' me.

EDWARD (*smiling*): All right, Mrs Johnstone. (*He puts the locket round his neck)*

He looks at her a moment too long.

MRS JOHNSTONE: What y' lookin' at?

EDWARD: I thought you didn't like me. I thought you weren't very nice. But I think you're smashing.

MRS JOHNSTONE (*looking at him*); God help the girls when you start dancing.

EDWARD: Pardon?

MRS JOHNSTON: Nothing. (*Calling into the house.*) Mickey, say goodbye to Eddie – he's moving.

MICKEY *comes out of the house.*

Music is quietly introduced.

EDDIE *moves to* MICKEY *and gives him a small parcel from his pocket.* MICKEY *unwraps a toy gun. The two boys clasp hands and wave goodbye.* MRS JOHNSTONE *and* MICKEY *watch as* EDWARD *joins his parents, dressed in outdoor clothes, on their side of the stage.*

EDWARD: Goodbye.

MR LYONS: Well, Edward . . . do you like it here?

EDWARD (*unenthusiastically*): It's very nice.

MRS LYONS: Oh, look, Edward . . . look at those trees and those cows. Oh Edward you're going to like it so much out here, aren't you?

EDWARD: Yes. Are you feeling better now, Mummy?

MRS LYONS: Much better now, darling. Oh Edward, look, look at those birds . . . Look at that lovely black and white one . . .

EDWARD (*immediately covering his eyes*): Don't Mummy, don't look. It's a magpie, never look at one magpie. It's one for sorrow . . .

MR LYONS: Edward . . . that's just stupid superstition.

EDWARD: It's not, Mickey told me.

MRS LYONS: Edward, I think we can forget the silly things that Mickey said.

EDWARD: I'm going inside. I want to read.

EDWARD *exits.*

MR LYONS (*comforting his wife*): Children take time to adapt to new surroundings. He'll be as right as rain in a few days. He won't even remember he once lived somewhere else.

MRS LYONS *forces a smile and allows herself to be led inside by her husband.*

MICKEY *rings the doorbell of* EDWARD*'s old house.*
A WOMAN *answers the door.*

WOMAN: Yes?

MICKEY: Is er . . . is Eddie in?

WOMAN: Eddie? I'm afraid Eddie doesn't live here now.

MICKEY: Oh, yeh. (*He stands looking at the woman.*)

WOMAN: Goodbye.

MICKEY: Do y' . . . erm, do y' know where he lives now?

WOMAN: Pardon?

MICKEY: See, I've got some money, I was gonna go, on the bus, an' see him. Where does he live now?

WOMAN: I'm afraid I've no idea.

MICKEY: It's somewhere in the country, isn't it?

WOMAN: Look, I honestly don't know and I'm rather busy. Goodbye.

The WOMAN *closes the door on* MICKEY.
MICKEY *wanders away, aimless and bored, deserted and alone.*
Music.

MICKEY (*singing*): No kids out on the street today,
You could be living on the moon.
Maybe everybody's packed their bags and moved away,
Gonna be a long, long, long,
Sunday Afternoon

Just killing time and kicking cans around,
Try to remember jokes I knew,
I tell them to myself, but they're not funny since I found
It's gonna be a long, long, long,
Sunday Afternoon.

EDWARD, *in his garden, equally bored and alone. The scene appears in such a way that we don't know if it is real or in* MICKEY*'s mind.*

My best friend
Always had sweets to share, (He)
Knew every word in the dictionary.
He was clean, neat and tidy,
From Monday to Friday,
I wish that I could be like,
Wear clean clothes, talk properly like,
Do sums and history like,

EDWARD } (*together*): My friend
MICKEY } My friend

EDWARD: My best friend
He could swear like a soldier
You would laugh till you died
At the stories he told y'
He was untidy
From Monday to Friday
I wish that I could be like
Kick a ball and climb a tree like
Run around with dirty knees like

EDWARD } (*together*): My friend
MICKEY } My friend

The Lights fade on EDWARD *as the music shifts back to 'Long Sunday Afternoon'.*

MICKEY: Feels like everybody stayed in bed
Or maybe I woke up too soon.
Am I the last survivor
Is everybody dead?
On this long long long
Sunday Afternoon.

MRS JOHNSTONE *appears, clutching a letter.*

MRS JOHNSTONE (*singing*): Oh, bright new day,
We're movin' away.

MICKEY (*speaking*): Mam? What's up?

MRS JOHNSTONE (*singing*): We're startin' all over again.

DONNA MARIE *enters together with various neighbours.*

DONNA MARIE (*speaking*): Is it a summons, Mother?

MRS JOHNSTONE (*singing*): Oh, bright new day,
We're goin' away.

MICKEY (*calling*): Sammy!

MRS JOHNSTONE *addresses the various onlookers.*

MRS JOHNSTONE (*singing*): Where nobody's heard of our name.

SAMMY *enters.*

SAMMY (*speaking*): I never robbed nothin', honest, mam.

MRS JOHNSTONE (*singing*): Where we can begin again,
Feel we can win and then
Live just like livin' should be
Got a new situation,
A new destination,
And no reputation following me.

MICKEY (*speaking*): What is it, what is it?

MRS JOHNSTONE (*singing*): We're gettin' out,
We're movin' house,
We're starting all over again.
We're leavin' this mess
For our new address (*pointing it out*)
'Sixty five Skelmersdale Lane'.

MICKEY (*speaking; worried*): Where's that, mam?

SAMMY (*speaking*): Is that in the country?

DONNA MARIE (*speaking*): What's it like there?

MRS JOHNSTONE (*singing*): The air is so pure,
You get drunk just by breathing,
And the washing stays clean on the line.
Where there's space for the kids,
'Cos the garden's so big,
It would take you a week just to reach the far side.

(*Speaking*): Come on, Sammy, Mickey, now you've all gorra help. (*To the* NEIGHBOURS, *in a 'posh' voice.*) Erm would youse excuse us, we've gorra pack. We're movin' away.

MRS JOHNSTONE *and the children go in to pack.*

NEIGHBOUR: What did she say?

MILKMAN: They're movin' away.

ALL: Praise the Lord, he has delivered us at last.

NEIGHBOUR: They're gettin' out,
They're movin' house,
Life won't be the same as in the past.

POLICEMAN: I can safely predict
A sharp drop in the crime rate.

NEIGHBOUR: It'll be calm an' peaceful around here.

MILKMAN: AND now I might even
Get paid what is mine, mate.

NEIGHBOUR: An' you'll see, grafitti will soon disappear.

MRS JOHNSTONE *marches out of the house carrying battered suitcases, followed by the children who are struggling to get out some of the items mentioned in the verse.*

MRS JOHNSTONE: Just pack up the bags,
We're leavin' the rags,
The wobbly wardrobe, chest of drawers that never close.
The two legged chair, the carpet so bare,
You wouldn't see it if it wasn't for the holes.
Now that we're movin'
Now that we're improvin',
Let's just wash our hands of this lot.

For it's no longer fitting, for me to be sitting
On a sofa, I know for a fact, was knocked off.

Her last line is delivered to SAMMY *who indicates the* POLICEMAN, *trying to get her to shut up.*

We might get a car,
Be all 'lardie dah',
An' go drivin' out to the sands.
At the weekend,
A gentleman friend,
Might take me dancing
To the local bands.
We'll have a front room,
And then if it should happen,
That His Holiness flies in from Rome,
He can sit there with me, eating toast, drinking tea
In the sort of surroundings that remind him of home.

MICKEY (*speaking*): It's like the country, isn't it, mam?

MRS JOHNSTONE (*speaking*): Ey, we'll be all right out here son, away from the muck an' the dirt an' the bloody trouble. Eh, I could dance. Come here.

MICKEY: Get off . . .

MRS JOHNSTONE *picks up a picture of the Pope which is lying next to one of the suitcases and begins to dance.*

MRS JOHNSTONE (*singing*): Oh, bright new day,
We're movin' away,
We're startin' all over again.
Oh, bright new day,
We're goin' away,
Where nobody's heard of our name.

(*Speaking*): An' what are you laughin' at?

MICKEY: I'm not laughin', I'm smilin'. I haven't seen you happy like this for ages.

MRS JOHNSTONE: Well, I am happy now. Eh, Jesus where's the others?

MICKEY: They went into that field, mam.

MRS JOHNSTONE: Sammy. SAMMY! Get off that bleedin' cow before I kill you. Oh Jesus, what's our Donna Marie stepped into? Sammy, that cow's a bull. Come here the pair of you.

Now we can begin again,
Feel we can win an' then,
Live just like livin' should be.
Got a new situation,

A new destination,
An' no reputation following me.

ALL: We're gettin' out. We're movin' house
We're goin' away. Gettin' out today.
We're movin' movin' movin' house.

MRS JOHNSTONE: We're goin' away,
Oh, bright new day.

Curtain.

ACT TWO

MRS JOHNSTONE *moves forward to sing.*

MRS JOHNSTONE: The house we got was lovely,
They neighbours are a treat,
They sometimes fight on Saturday night,
But never in the week.

MRS JOHNSTONE *turns and looks 'next door'. Raised voices, and a dog barking, are heard, off.*

NEIGHBOURS (*off, speaking*): What time do you call this then?
Time I got shot of you, rat bag!

DOG *barks.*

MRS JOHNSTONE (*singing*): Since I pay me bills on time, the milkman
Insists I call him Joe.
He brings me bread and eggs.

JOE, *the milkman, enters.*

Says I've got legs
Like Marilyn Monroe.

MRS JOHNSTONE *and* JOE *dance.*

Sometimes he takes me dancing
Even takes me dancing.

JOE *exits, dancing.*

I know our Sammy burnt the school down
But it's very easily done.
If the teacher lets the silly gets
Play with magnesium.
Thank God he only got probation,

A JUDGE *is seen, ticking* SAMMY *off.*

The Judge was old and slow.

MRS JOHNSTONE *sings to the* JUDGE, *laying on a smile for him.*

Though it was kind of him,
Said I reminded him of Marilyn Monroe.

JUDGE (*slightly scandalized*): And could I take you dancing?
Take you dancing.

MRS JOHNSTONE *takes the* JUDGE*'s gavel and bangs him on the head.*

The JUDGE *exits, stunned.*

MRS JOHNSTONE: Our Mickey's just turned fourteen
Y' know he's at *that* age

MICKEY *is seen in his room.*

When you mention girls, or courting,

He flies into a rage.

MICKEY (*speaking*): Shut up talking about me, Mother.

MRS JOHNSTONE: He's got a thing for taking blackheads out,
And he thinks that I don't know,
That he dreams all night of girls who look like
Marilyn Monroe. He's even started dancing, secret dancing.
(*Slower*): And as for the rest, they've flown the nest
Got married or moved away
Our Donna Marie's already got three, she's
A bit like me that way . . .
(*Slower*): And that other child of mine,
I haven't seen for years, although
Each day I pray he'll be OK,
Not like Marilyn Monroe . . .

On the other side of the stage MRS LYONS *enters, waltzing with a very awkward fourteen-year-old* EDWARD.

MRS LYONS (*speaking*): One, two, three. One, two three.
(*Singing*): Yes, that's right, you're dancing.
That's right, you're dancing.
(*Speaking*): You see, Edward, it is easy.

EDWARD: It is if you have someone to practice with. Girls. But in term time we hardly ever see a girl, let alone dance with one.

MRS LYONS: I'll give you some more lessons when you're home for half term. Now come on, come on, you're going to be late. Daddy's at the door with the car. Now, are you sure you've got all your bags?

EDWARD: Yes, they're in the boot.

MRS LYONS (*looking at him*): I'll see you at half term then, darling. (*She kisses him, a light kiss, but holds on to him.*) Look after yourself my love.

EDWARD: Oh Mummy . . . stop fussing . . . I'm going to be late.

MRS LYONS: We have had a very good time this holiday though, haven't we?

EDWARD: We always do.

MRS LYONS: Yes. We're safe here, aren't we?

EDWARD: Mummy what are you on about? Sometimes . . .
A car horn is heard.

MRS LYONS (*hustling him out, good naturedly*): Go on, go on . . . There's Daddy getting impatient. Bye, bye, Edward.

EDWARD: Bye, Ma.
EDWARD *exits.*

We see MRS JOHNSTONE *hustling* MICKEY *to school.*

MRS JOHNSTONE: You're gonna be late y' know. Y' late already.

MICKEY: I'm not.

MRS JOHNSTONE: You're gonna miss the bus.

MICKEY: I won't.

MRS JOHNSTONE: Well, you'll miss Linda, she'll be waitin' for y'.

MICKEY: Well, I don't wanna see her. What do I wanna see her for?

MRS JOHNSTONE (*laughing at his transparency*): You've only been talkin' about her in your sleep for the past week . . .

MICKEY (*outraged*): You liar . . .

MRS JOHNSTONE: 'Oh, my sweet darling . . .'

MICKEY: I never. That was – a line out the school play!

MRS JOHNSTONE (*her laughter turning to a smile*): All right. I believe y'. Now go before you miss the bus. Are y' goin'.

We see LINDA *at the bus stop.*

LINDA: Hi-ya, Mickey.

MRS JOHNSTONE: Ogh, did I forget? Is that what you're waitin' for? Y' waitin' for y' mum to give y' a big sloppy kiss, come here . . .

MICKEY: I'm goin', I'm goin' . . .

SAMMY *runs through the house, pulling on a jacket as he does so.*

SAMMY: Wait for me, YOU.

MRS JOHNSTONE: Where you goin' Sammy?

SAMMY (*on his way out*): The dole.

MICKEY *and* SAMMY *exit.*

MRS JOHNSTONE *stands watching them as they approach the bus stop. She smiles at* MICKEY*'s failure to cope with* LINDA*'s smile of welcome.*

The 'bus' appears, with the NARRATOR *as the conductor.*

CONDUCTOR: Come on, if y' gettin' on. We've not got all day.

SAMMY, MICKEY *and* LINDA *get on the 'bus'.*

MRS JOHNSTONE (*calling to her kids*): Tarrah, lads. Be good, both of y' now. I'll cook a nice surprise for y' tea.

CONDUCTOR (*noticing her as he goes to ring the bell*): Gettin' on, Missis?

MRS JOHNSTONE *shakes her head, still smiling.*

(*Speaking*): Happy are y'. Content at last?
Wiped out what happened, forgotten the past?
She looks at him, puzzled.
But you've got to have an endin', if a start's been made.
No one gets off without the price bein' paid.
The 'bus' pulls away as the conductor begins to collect fares.
No one can embark without the price bein' paid.
(*To* MICKEY): Yeh?

MICKEY (*handing over his money*): A fourpenny scholar.

CONDUCTOR: How old are y'?

LINDA: He's fourteen. Both of us are. A fourpenny scholar for me as well.

The CONDUCTOR *gives out the ticket as* SAMMY *offers his money.*

SAMMY: Same for me.

CONDUCTOR: No son.

SAMMY: What?

CONDUCTOR: You're older than fourteen.

MICKEY (*worried*): Sammy . . .

SAMMY: Shut it. (*To the* CONDUCTOR.) I'm fourteen. I wanna fourpenny scholar.

CONDUCTOR: Do you know the penalty for tryin' to defraud . . .

SAMMY: I'm not defraudin' no one.

CONDUCTOR (*shouting to the* DRIVER): 'Ey, Billy, take the next left will y'. We've got one for the cop shop here.

SAMMY: What? (*He stands.*)

MICKEY: He didn't mean it, Mister. Don't be soft. He, he was jokin'. Sammy tell him, tell him you're really sixteen. I'll lend you the rest of the fare . . .

SAMMY (*considers; then*): Fuck off. (*He produces a knife. To the* CONDUCTOR.) Now move, you. Move! Give me the bag.

Music.

MICKEY: Sammy . . . Sammy . . .

SAMMY (*to the* CONDUCTOR): I said give. Stop the bus.
The CONDUCTOR *rings the bell to stop the 'bus'.*
Come on, Mickey.

LINDA: You stay where y' are, Mickey. You've done nothin'.

MICKEY: Sammy, Sammy put that away . . . it's still not too late. (*To the* CONDUCTOR.) Is it Mister?

SAMMY: Mickey.

LINDA: He's stayin' here.

SAMMY: No-mark!

SAMMY *leaps from the 'bus' and is pursued by two policemen. The 'bus' pulls away leaving* MICKEY *and* LINDA *alone on the pavement.*

LINDA: He'll get put away for this, y' know, Mickey.

MICKEY: I know.

LINDA: He's always been a soft get, your Sammy.

MICKEY: I know.

LINDA: You better hadn't do anything soft, like him.

MICKEY: I wouldn't.

LINDA: Y' better hadn't or I won't be in love with y' anymore!

MICKEY: Shut up! Y' always sayin' that.

LINDA: I'm not.

MICKEY: Yis y' are. Y' bloody well said it in assembly yesterday.

LINDA: Well. I was only tellin' y'.

MICKEY: Yeh, an' five hundred others as well.

LINDA: I don't care who knows. I just love you. I love you!

MICKEY: Come on . . . we're half an hour late as it is.

MICKEY *hurries off, followed by* LINDA.

EDWARD*'s school where* EDWARD *is confronted by a teacher (the* NARRATOR*) looking down his nose at* EDWARD.

TEACHER: You're doing very well here, aren't you, Lyons?

EDWARD: Yes, sir. I believe so.

TEACHER: Talk of Oxbridge.

EDWARD: Yes, sir.

TEACHER: Getting rather big for your boots, aren't you?

EDWARD: No, sir.

TEACHER: No, sir? Yes, sir. I think you're a tyke, Lyons. The boys in your dorm say you wear a locket around your neck. Is that so?

Pause.

EDWARD: Yes, sir.

TEACHER: A locket? A locket. This is a boys' school, Lyons.

EDWARD: I am a boy, sir.

TEACHER: They you must behave like one. Now give this locket to me.

EDWARD: No, sir.

TEACHER: No sir? Am I to punish you Lyons? Am I to have you flogged?

EDWARD: You can do exactly as you choose Sir. You can take a flying fuck at a rolling doughnut! But you shall not take my locket!

TEACHER (*thunderstruck*): I'm going to . . . I'm going to have you suspended, Lyons.

EDWARD: Yes, sir.

EDWARD *exits.*

As EDWARD *exits a class in a Secondary Modern school is formed – all boredom and futility. The school bell rings. The teacher becomes the teacher of this class in which we see* LINDA *and* MICKEY.

TEACHER: And so, we know then, don't we, that the Boro Indian of the Amazon Basin lives on a diet of . . .

PERKINS: Sir, sir . . .

TEACHER: A diet of . . .

PERKINS: Sir, sir . . .

TEACHER: A diet of what, Johnstone? The Boro Indian of the Amazon Basin lives on a diet of what?

MICKEY: What?

TEACHER: Exactly lad, exactly. What?

MICKEY: I don't know.

TEACHER (*his patience gone*): Y' don't know. (*Mimicking.*) You don't know. I told y' two minutes ago, lad.

LINDA: Leave him alone will y'.

TEACHER: You just stay out of this, Miss. It's got nothing to do with you. It's Johnstone, not you . . .

PERKINS: Sir!

TEACHER: Oh, shut up Perkins, y' borin' little turd. But you don't listen do you, Johnstone?

MICKEY (*shrugging*): Yeh.

TEACHER: Oh, y' do? Right, come out here in front of the class. Now then, what is the staple diet of the Boro Indian of the Amazon Basin?

MICKEY *looks about for help. There is none.*

MICKEY (*defiantly*): Fish Fingers!

TEACHER: Just how the hell do you hope to get a job when you never listen to anythin'?

MICKEY: It's borin'.

TEACHER: Yes, yes, you might think it's boring but you won't be sayin' that when you can't get a job.

MICKEY: Yeh. Yeh an' it'll really help me to get a job if I know what some soddin' pygmies in Africa have for their dinner!

The class erupts into laughter.

TEACHER (*to class*): Shut up. Shut up.

MICKEY: Or maybe y' were thinkin' I was lookin' for a job in an African restaurant.

TEACHER: Out!

LINDA: Take no notice Mickey. I love you.

TEACHER: Johnstone, get out!

LINDA: Oh, leave him alone you. Y' big worm!

TEACHER: Right you as well . . . out . . . out . . .

LINDA: I'm goin' . . . I'm goin' . . .

TEACHER: You're both suspended.

LINDA *and* MICKEY *leave the class.*

The classroom sequence breaks up as we see MRS LYONS *staring at a piece of paper.* EDWARD *is standing before her.*

MRS LYONS (*incredulously*): Suspended? Suspended? (*She looks at the paper.*) Because of a locket?

EDWARD: Because I wouldn't let them have my locket.

MRS LYONS: But what's so . . . Can I see this locket?

There is a pause.

EDWARD: I suppose so . . . if you want to.

EDWARD *takes off the locket from around his neck and hands it to his mother. She looks at it without opening it.*

MRS LYONS: Where did you get this?

EDWARD: I can't tell you that. It's a secret.

MRS LYONS (*finally smiling in relief*): I know it's from a girlfriend, isn't it? (*She laughs.*) Is there a picture in here?

EDWARD: Yes, Mummy. Can I have it back now?

MRS LYONS: You won't let Mummy see your girl friend. Oh, Edward, don't be so . . . (*She playfully moves away.*) Is she beautiful?

EDWARD: Mummy can . . .

MRS LYONS: Oh, let me look, let me look. (*She beams a smile at him and then opens the locket.*)

Music.

EDWARD: Mummy . . . Mummy what's wrong . . . (*He goes to her and holds her steady.*) Mummy!

MRS LYONS *takes his arms away from her.*

What is it?

MRS LYONS: When . . . when were you photographed with this woman?

EDWARD: Pardon!

MRS LYONS: When! Tell me, Edward.

EDWARD *begins to laugh.*

Edward!

EDWARD: Mummy . . . you silly old thing. That's not me. That's Mickey.

MRS LYONS: What?

EDWARD: Mickey . . . you remember my friend when I was little. (*He takes the locket and shows it to her.*) Look. That's Mickey . . . and his mother. Why did you think it was me? (*He looks at it.*) I never looked a bit like Mickey.

EDWARD *replaces the locket around his neck.* MRS LYONS *watches him.*

MRS LYONS: No it's just . . . (*She stares, deep in thought.*)

EDWARD (*looking at her*): Are you feeling all right Mummy? You're not ill again, like you used to be . . . are you?

MRS LYONS: Where did you get that . . . locket from, Edward? Why do you wear it?

EDWARD: I can't tell you that, Ma. I've explained, it's a secret, I can't tell you.

MRS LYONS: But . . . but I'm your mother.

EDWARD: I know but I still can't tell you. It's not important, I'm going up to my room. It's just a secret, everybody has secrets, don't you have secrets?

EDWARD *exits to his room.*

The NARRATOR *enters.*

Music (continues).

NARRATOR (*singing*): Did you really feel that you'd become secure
That time had brushed away the past
That there's no one by the window, no one knocking on your door
Did you believe that you were free at last
Free from the broken looking glass.

Oh y' know the devil's got your number

He's never far behind you
He always knows where to find you
And someone said they'd seen him walking past your door.

NARRATOR *exits.*

We see MICKEY *and* LINDA *making their way up the hill.* LINDA *having some difficulty in high heeled shoes.*

LINDA: Tch . . . you didn't tell me it was gonna be over a load of fields.

MICKEY: I didn't tell y' nothin'. I didn't ask y' to come, y' followed me. (*He walks away from her.*)

LINDA (*watching him walk away*): Mickey, Mickey . . . I'm stuck . . . (*Holding out her helpless arms.*) Me foot's stuck. Honest.

MICKEY *goes back, timidly takes a wrist and ineffectually pulls.*

Mickey, I think y' might be more successful if you were to sort of put your arms around here. (*She puts her hands on her waist.*) Oh Mickey, be gentle, be gentle . . .

MICKEY (*managing to pull her free*): Will you stop takin' the piss out of me!

LINDA: I'm not, I'm not.

MICKEY *points down in the direction they have come from.*

MICKEY: Look . . . y' can see the estate from up here.

LINDA: Have we come all this way just to look at the bleedin' estate? Mickey we're fourteen.

She beams at him. He can't take it and looks the other way.

MICKEY: Look.

LINDA: What?

MICKEY: There's that lad lookin' out the window. I see him sometimes when I'm up here.

LINDA: Oh him . . . he's gorgeous, isn't he?

MICKEY: What?

LINDA: He's lovely lookin', isn't he?

MICKEY: All right, all right! You've told me once.

LINDA: Well, he is. An' what do you care if I think another feller's gorgeous eh?

MICKEY: I don't.

LINDA: You . . . I give up with you, Mickey Johnstone. I'm off. You get on my bleedin' nerves.

LINDA *exits.*

MICKEY: What . . . Linda . . . Linda . . . Don't . . . Linda, I wanna kiss y', an' put me arms around y' an' kiss y' and kiss y' an even fornicate with y' but I don't know how to tell y', because I've got pimples an' me feet are too big an' me bum sticks out an' . . .

He becomes conscious of EDWARD *approaching, and affects nonchalance.*

(*Speaking*): If I was like him
I'd know (*singing*) all the right words

EDWARD: If I was like . . . him
I'd know some real birds
Apart from those in my dreams
And in magazines.

MICKEY: Just look at his hair

EDWARD: His hair's dark and wavy
Mine's mousey to fair

MICKEY: Mine's the colour of gravy

EDWARD
MICKEY } (*together*): Each part of his face
Is in just the right place
He laughing at me
At my nose, did he notice

MICKEY: I should wear a brace

EDWARD: That I've got halitosis

MICKEY
EDWARD } (*together*): When nature picked on me
She chose to stick on me

EDWARD: Eyes that don't match

MICKEY: And ears that stand out

EDWARD
MICKEY } (*together*): She picked the wrong batch
When she handed mine out
And then she attacked me
With permanent acne

EDWARD: I wish I was a bit like
Wish that I could score a hit like
And be just a little bit like
That guy
That guy

MICKEY: I wish that I could be like
Just a little less like me
Like the sort of guy I see, like
That guy
That guy.

EDWARD: Hi.

MICKEY: Hi. Gis a ciggie?

EDWARD: Oh, I don't smoke actually. But I can go and get

you some.

MICKEY: Are you soft? (*He suddenly realizes.*) A blood brother.

EDWARD: Mickey? Well, shag the vicar.

MICKEY *laughs.*

What's wrong?

MICKEY: You, it sounds dead funny swearin' in that posh voice.

EDWARD: What posh voice?

MICKEY: That one.

EDWARD: Well, where do you live?

MICKEY: The estate, look. (*He points.*)

EDWARD: My God, I only live . . .

MICKEY: I know.

EDWARD: That girl I saw you with, was that . . .

MICKEY: Linda. Do you remember Linda?

EDWARD: Wow, was that Linda? And is she your girl friend?

MICKEY: Yeh. She's one of them.

EDWARD: One of them.

MICKEY: Have you got a girl friend?

EDWARD: Me? Me? No!

MICKEY: Haven't y'?

EDWARD: Look, you seem to have rather a lot of them, erm . . . perhaps you'd share one with me.

MICKEY: Share one. Eddie I haven't even got one girl friend.

EDWARD: But Linda . . . you said . . .

MICKEY: I know, but she's not. I mean, I mean she would be me girl friend, she even says she loves me all over the place, but it's just like dead difficult.

EDWARD: What?

MICKEY: Like knowing what to say.

EDWARD: But you must, you must . . .

MICKEY: I know that. But every time I see her I promise meself I'll ask her but, but the words just disappear.

EDWARD: But you mustn't let them.

MICKEY: What do I say, though?

EDWARD: Mickey, it's easy, I've read about it. Look the next time you see Linda, you stare straight into her eyes and you say, 'Linda, I love you, I want you, the very core of my being is longing for you, my loins are burning for you. Let me lay my weary head between your warm breasts'! And then,

Mickey, her eyes will be half closed and her voice may appear somewhat husky as she pleads with you, 'be gentle with me, be gentle'.' It would work, you know. Listen, we can see how it's done; look the Essoldo for one week only, *Nymphomaniac Nights* and *Swedish Au Pairs*. Whoa . . .

MICKEY: I'll have to go home and get some money . . .

As the boys are going, we see MRS LYONS *appear. She has seen* EDWARD *and* MICKEY *and she stares after them. Making up her mind she quickly goes and fetches a coat, then follows the two boys.*

The NARRATOR *enters.*

Music.

EDWARD: I've got plenty, I'll lend . . .

MICKEY: No, it's all right, me Mam'll give it me . . .

EDWARD: Come on then, before my Ma sees me. She's off her beam, my Ma . . .

The boys exit, followed by MRS LYONS.

NARRATOR (*singing*): Did you really feel that you'd become secure,
And that the past was tightly locked away,
Did you really feel that you would never be found,
Did you forget you've got some debts to pay,
Did you forget about the reckoning day.

Yes, the devil he's still got your number,
He's moved in down the street from you,
Someone said he wants to speak to you,
Someone said they'd seen him leanin' on your door.

The NARRATOR *exits.*

We see MRS JOHNSTONE *in her kitchen as* MICKEY *bursts in followed by* EDWARD.

MICKEY: Mother, mam, look, look it's Eddie . . . Eddie . . .

MRS JOHNSTONE *stands looking at* EDWARD *and smiling.*

EDWARD: Hi-ya, Mrs Johnstone. Isn't it fantastic. We're neighbours again.

MICKEY: Mum, mum, mum, Eddie lives in that house, y' know that big house on the hill. Mam, can y' lend us a quid to go to the pictures . . .

MRS JOHNSTONE: Yes, it's, erm . . . it's in the sideboard . . .

MICKEY: Oh thanks, mam. I love y'.

MICKEY *exits to the next room.*

EDWARD: You're looking very well, Mrs Johnstone.

MRS JOHNSTONE: Am I? Do you . . . Do you still keep that locket I gave y'?

EDWARD: Of course . . . Look . . .

MICKEY *enters.*

MICKEY: Mam, Mam, can I bring Eddie back afterwards, for coffee?

MRS JOHNSTONE: Yeh. Go on . . . go an' enjoy yourselves but don't be too late will y'?

MICKEY: See y', Mam . . .

EDWARD: Bye Mrs Johnstone.

The boys prepare to leave.

MRS JOHNSTONE: 'Ey. What's the film you're gonna see?

EDWARD: Erm what?

MRS JOHNSTONE: What film . . .

EDWARD } (*together*): *Dr Zhivago*
MICKEY } *Magnificent Seven*

MRS JOHNSTONE: Dr Zhivago's Magnificent Seven.

EDWARD: It's a double bill.

MRS JOHNSTONE: I see. An' where's it on?

MICKEY } (*together*): WHAT?
EDWARD } The Essoldo

MRS JOHNSTONE: Oh . . . the Essoldo eh? When I passed the Essoldo this mornin' they were showin' *Nymphomaniac Nights* and *Swedish Au Pairs.*

EDWARD: Ah yes, Mrs Johnstone, yes, yes they're just the trailers: a documentary and and . . .

MICKEY: An' a travelogue. About Sweden!

MRS JOHNSTONE: Do the pair of you really think I was born yesterday?

EDWARD *can't hold it any longer and breaks into embarrassed laughter.*

MICKEY (*trying to hold on*): It is, it is . . . it's just a travelogue . . .

MRS JOHNSTONE: Showing the spectacular bends and curves of Sweden . . . Go on y' randy little sods . . .

MICKEY (*scandalized*): Mother!

MRS JOHNSTONE: Go on before I throw a bucket of water over the pair of y' . . .

MICKEY *drags* EDWARD *out.*

I don't know about coffee . . . you'd be better off with bromide. (*She gets on with her work.*)

EDWARD (*outside the house but looking back*): She's fabulous your ma, isn't she?

MICKEY: She's a fuckin' head case. Come on . . .

As they run off we see MRS LYONS *appear from where she has been concealed in the alley.*

MRS JOHNSTONE *is lilting the 'We Go Dancing' line as* MRS LYONS *appears in the kitchen.* MRS JOHNSTONE *gets a shock as she looks up and sees* MRS LYONS *there. The two women stare at each other.*

MRS JOHNSTONE (*eventually nodding*): Hello.

MRS LYONS: How long have you lived here?

Pause.

MRS JOHNSTONE: A few years.

Pause.

MRS LYONS: Are you always going to follow me?

MRS JOHNSTONE: We were rehoused here . . . I didn't follow . . .

MRS LYONS: Don't lie! I know what you're doing to me! You gave him that locket didn't you? Mm?

MRS JOHNSTONE *nods.*

He never takes it off you know. You're very clever aren't you?

MRS JOHNSTONE: I . . . I thought I'd never see him again. I wanted him to have . . . a picture of me . . . even though he'd never know.

MRS LYONS: Afraid he might eventually have forgotten you? Oh no. There's no chance of that. He'll always remember you. After we'd moved he talked less and less of you and your family. I started . . . just for a while I came to believe that he was actually mine.

MRS JOHNSTONE: He is yours.

MRS LYONS: No. I took him. But I never made him mine. Does he know? Have you told . . .

MRS JOHNSTONE: Of course not!

MRS LYONS: Even when – when he was a tiny baby I'd see him looking straight at me and I'd think, he knows . . . he knows. (*Pause.*) You have ruined me. (*Pause.*) But you won't ruin Edward! Is it money you want?

MRS JOHNSTONE: What?

MRS LYONS: I'll get it for you. If you move away from here. How much?

MRS JOHNSTONE: Look . . .

MRS LYONS: How much?

MRS JOHNSTONE: Nothin'! Nothing. (*Pause.*) You bought me off once before . . .

MRS LYONS: Thousands . . . I'm talking about thousands if you want it. And think what you could do with money like that.

MRS JOHNSTONE: I'd spend it. I'd buy more junk and trash; that's all. I don't want your money. I've made a life out here. It's not much of one maybe, but I made it. I'm stayin' here. You move if you want to.

MRS LYONS: I would. But there's no point. You'd just follow me again wouldn't you?

MRS JOHNSTONE: Look I'm not followin' anybody.

MRS LYONS: Wherever I go you'll be just behind me. I know that now . . . always and forever and ever like, like a shadow . . . unless I can . . . make . . . you go . . . But you won't so . . .

We see that throughout the above MRS LYONS *has opened the knife drawer and has a lethal-looking kitchen knife in her hand.* MRS JOHNSTONE, *unaware, has her back to her. On impulse, and punctuated by a note,* MRS JOHNSTONE *wheels. On a punctuated note* MRS LYONS *lunges.* MRS JOHNSTONE *moves and avoids it.* MRS LYONS *lunges again but* MRS JOHNSTONE *manages to get hold of her wrist, rendering the knife hand helpless.* MRS JOHNSTONE *takes the knife from* MRS LYON*'s grasp and moves away.*

MRS JOHNSTONE (*staring at her; knowing*): YOU'RE MAD. MAD.

MRS LYONS (*quietly*): I curse the day I met you. You ruined me.

MRS JOHNSTONE: Go. Just go!

MRS LYONS: Witch. (*Suddenly pointing.*) I curse you. Witch!

MRS JOHNSTONE (*screaming*): Go!

MRS LYONS *exits to the street.*

KIDS *voices are heard, chanting, off.*

KIDS (*off*): High upon the hill the mad woman lives,
Never ever eat the sweets she gives,
Just throw them away and tell your Dad,
High upon a hill there's a woman gone mad.

Mad woman, mad woman living on the hill,
If she catches your eye then you never will

Grow any further, your teeth will go bad
High upon a hill there's a woman gone mad.

EDDIE *and* MICKEY *emerge from the cinema, blinking as they try to adjust to the glare of the light in the street.*

They are both quite overcome with their celluloid/erotic encounter. As they pause and light up cigarettes by a corner lamp post they groan in their ecstatic agony. Each is in an aroused trance.

MICKEY: Ooh . . . !

EDWARD: Naked knockers, ooh . . . !

MICKEY: Naked knockers with nipples . . .

EDWARD: Playing tennis. Ooh. Tennis with tits. Will Wimbledon ever be the same?

MICKEY: Tits!

EDWARD: Tits, tits, tits . . . (*He begins a frustrated chant of the word, oblivious to everything.*)

LINDA *and a mate enter.*

Finally MICKEY *realizes* LINDA*'s presence and knocks* EDWARD, *who becomes aware of the girls' presence. He goes into a song without missing a beat.*

Tits, tits, tits a lovely way,
To spend an evening . . .

EDWARD *grabs* LINDA*'s mate and begins to waltz her around the street.*

Can't think of anything
I'd rather do . . .

MATE (*simultaneously with the above*): Gerroff. Put me down, get y' friggin' paws off me you. Linda. Y' bloody lunatic, gettoff.

EDWARD *finally releases her and bows.*

Linda, come on. I'm goin' . . .

The MATE *begins to walk away.* LINDA *makes no attempt to follow.*

LINDA: What y' doin' in town, Mick?

MICKEY: We've erm, we've . . .

EDWARD: We have been undergoing a remarkable celluloid experience!

MATE: We'll miss the bus, Linda.

MICKEY: We've been the pictures.

LINDA: So have we. What did y' go see?

EDWARD: *Nympho . . .*

MICKEY: *Bridge Over the River Kwai.*

LINDA: Ah, we've seen that. We went to see *Nymphomaniac Nights* instead. An' *Swedish Au Pairs.*

MICKEY: You what!

EDWARD *begins to laugh.*

MATE: Oh, sod y' then. I'm goin'.

The MATE *exits.*

MICKEY (*to* EDWARD): What are you laughin' at? Take no notice. Remember Eddie? He's still a head case. Shurrup.

EDWARD (*shouting*): Tits. Tits, tits, tits, tits, tits.

EDWARD *leaps around and hopefully ends up sitting at the top of the lamp post.* LINDA *and* MICKEY *laugh at him, while* EDWARD *chants.*

A POLICEMAN *enters.*

The three do not see the arrival of the POLICEMAN.

POLICEMAN: An' what the bloody hell do you think you're doin'?

EDWARD: Adolph Hitler?

POLICEMAN: Get down.

EDWARD *gets down from the lamp post.*

POLICEMAN (*getting out his black book*): Right. I want your names. What's your name?

LINDA:
MICKEY: } (*together*): Waitin' for the ninety-two bus!
EDWARD:

LINDA (*pointing upwards*): Oh my God, look . . .

POLICEMAN: Now listen . . .

The POLICEMAN *falls for it and looks up.*

The three make their exit.

The POLICEMAN *realizes and gives chase.*

MICKEY, LINDA *and* EDWARD *enter, laughing and exhausted.*

The NARRATOR *enters.*

NARRATOR: There's a few bob in your pocket and you've got good friends,
And it seems that Summer's never coming to an end,
Young, free and innocent, you haven't got a care,
Apart from decidin' on the clothes you're gonna wear.
The street's turned into Paradise, the radio's singing dreams
You're innocent, immortal, you're just fifteen.

The NARRATOR *becomes the rifle range man at the fairground.*

LINDA, MICKEY *and* EDWARD *rush on.*

LINDA, MICKEY *and* EDWARD *pool their money and hand it to the rifle range man. He gives the gun to* MICKEY, *who smiles, shakes his head and points to* LINDA. *The man offers the gun to* EDWARD *but* LINDA *takes it. The boys indicate to the rifle range man that he has had it now* LINDA *has the gun. They eagerly watch the target but their smiles fade as* LINDA *misses all three shots.* MICKEY *and* EDWARD *turn on* LINDA *in mock anger. They are stopped by the rifle range man throwing them a coconut which is used as a ball for a game of piggy-in-the-middle. When* LINDA *is caught in the middle the game freezes.*

And who'd dare tell the lambs in Spring,
What fate the later seasons bring.
Who'd tell the girl in the middle of the pair
The price she'll pay for just being there.

Throughout the following we see LINDA, MICKEY *and* EDWARD *suiting their action to the words – coming out of the chip shop, talking, lighting a cigarette by the lamp post.*

But leave them alone, let them go and play
They care not for what's at the end of the day.
For what is to come, for what might have been,
Life has no ending when you're sweet sixteen
And your friends are with you to talk away the night,
Or until Mrs Wong switches off the chippy light.
Then there's always the corner and the street lamp's glare
An' another hour to spend, with your friends, with her,
To share your last cigarette and your secret dream
At the midnight hour, at seventeen.

Throughout the following we see LINDA, MICKEY *and* EDWARD, *as if at the beach,* LINDA *taking a picture of* MICKEY *and* EDWARD, *arms around each other camping it for the camera but eventually giving good and open smiles.* MICKEY *taking a picture of* EDWARD *and* LINDA. EDWARD *down on one knee and kissing her hand* EDWARD *taking a picture of* MICKEY *and* LINDA. MICKEY *pulling a distorted face,* LINDA *wagging a finger at him.* MICKEY *chastened.* LINDA *raising her eyebrows and putting one of his arms round her.* LINDA *moving forward and taking the camera.* LINDA *waving the* NARRATOR *to snap them. He goes.* LINDA *showing the* NARRATOR *how to operate the camera.* LINDA, MICKEY *and* EDWARD, *grouped together, arms around each other as the* NARRATOR *takes the picture. They get the camera and wave their thanks to the* NARRATOR.

It's just another ferry boat, a trip to the beach
But everything is possible, the world's within your reach
An' you don't even notice broken bottles in the sand
The oil in the water and you can't understand
How living could be anything other than a dream
When you're young, free and innocent and just eighteen.

LINDA, MICKEY *and* EDWARD *exit.*

And only if the three of them could stay like that forever,
And only if we could predict no changes in the weather,
And only if we didn't live in life, as well as dreams
And only if we could stop and be forever, just eighteen.

We see EDWARD, *waiting by a street lamp.*
LINDA *approaches, sees him, and goes into a street walk.*

LINDA: Well, hallo, sweetie pie; looking for a good time? Ten to seven (*She laughs.*) Good time . . . ten to seven . . . it was a joke . . . I mean I know it was a lousy joke but y' could at least go into hysterics!

EDWARD *smiles.*

That's hysterics?

EDWARD: Where's Mickey?

LINDA: He must be workin' overtime.

EDWARD: Oh.

LINDA: What's wrong with you, misery?

EDWARD (*after a pause*): I go away to university tomorrow.

LINDA: Tomorrow! You didn't say.

EDWARD: I know. I think I've been pretending that if I didn't mention it the day would never come. I love it when we're together, the three of us, don't you?

LINDA *nods.*

Can I write to you?

LINDA: Yeh . . . yeh, if you want.

EDWARD: Would Mickey mind?

LINDA: Why should he?

EDWARD: Come on . . . because you're his girl friend.

LINDA: No, I'm not.

EDWARD: You are, Linda.

LINDA: I'm not, he hasn't asked me.

EDWARD (*laughing*): You mean he still hasn't?

LINDA (*laughing*): No.

EDWARD: But it's ridiculous.

LINDA: I know. I hope for his sake he never has to ask me to marry him. He'll be a pensioner before he gets around to it.

EDWARD (*after a pause*): He's mad. If I was Mickey I would have asked you years ago.

LINDA: I know *you* would. Cos y· soft you are.

EDWARD (*singing*): If I could stand inside his shoes I'd say,
How can I compare thee to a summer's day

LINDA (*speaking*): Oh go away . . .

EDWARD: I'd take a page in all the papers, I'd announce it on the news
If I was the guy, if I
Was in his shoes.

If I was him I'd bring you flowers
And ask you to dance
We'd while away the hours making future plans
For rainy days in country lanes
And trips to the sea
I'd just tell you that I love you
If it was me.

But I'm not saying a word,
I'm not saying I care,
Though I would like you to know,
That I'm not saying a word,
I'm not saying I care,
Though I would like you to know.

If I was him I'd have to tell you,
What I've kept in my heart,
That even if we had to live
Some worlds apart
There would not be a day
In which I'd not think of you
If I was him, if I was him
That's what I'd do.

But I'm not saying a word
I'm not saying I care
Though I would like you to know
That I'm not saying a word
I'm not saying I care
Though I would like you to know.

EDWARD: But I'm not.

LINDA: What?

EDWARD: Mickey.

MICKEY enters.

Mickey!

MICKEY: Hi-ya, Ed. Lind.

LINDA: Where've y' been?

MICKEY: I had to do overtime. I hate that soddin' place.

EDWARD: Mickey. I'm going away tomorrow . . . to University.

MICKEY: What? Y' didn't say.

EDWARD: I know . . . but the thing is I won't be back until Christmas. Three months. Now you wouldn't want me to continue in suspense for all that time would you?

LINDA: What are you on about?

EDDIE: Will you talk to Linda.

LINDA: Oh Eddie . . .

EDWARD: Go on . . . go on.

MICKEY *turns and goes to her.* LINDA *tries to keep a straight face.*

MICKEY: Erm . . . well, the er thing is . . . Linda, I've erm . . . (*Quickly.*) Linda for Christ's sake will you go out with me?

LINDA (*just as quickly*): Yeh.

MICKEY: Oh . . . erm . . . Good. Well, I suppose I better . . . well er . . . come here . . . (*He quickly embraces and kisses* LINDA.)

LINDA (*fighting for air*): My God. Y' take y' time gettin' goin' but then there's no stoppin' y'.

MICKEY: I know . . . come here . . .

They kiss again. EDWARD *turns and begins to leave.*

Eddie . . . Eddie where y' goin'? I though we were all goin' the club. There's a dance.

EDWARD: No . . . I've got to, erm, I've got to pack for tomorrow.

MICKEY: Are y' sure?

EDWARD *nods.*

See y' at Christmas then, Eddie? Listen, I'm gonna do loads of overtime between now and then, so the Christmas party's gonna be on me . . . right?

EDWARD: Right. It's a deal, Mick. See you.

LINDA *rushes across and kisses* EDWARD *lightly.*

LINDA: Thanks Eddie.

MICKEY: Yeh, Eddie . . . thanks.

LINDA *and* MICKEY, *arms around each other, watch him go. They turn and look at each other.*

MICKEY *and* LINDA *exit.*

The Lights crossfade to the JOHNSTONE *house.*

MICKEY *enters and prepares to go to work.*

MRS JOHNSTONE *enters with* MICKEY*'s lunch bag.*

The NARRATOR *enters.*

It was one day in October when the sun began to fade,
And Winter broke the promise that Summer had just made,
It was one day in October when the rain came falling down,
And someone said the bogey man was seen around the
town.

The NARRATOR *exits.*

MRS JOHNSTONE: Y' gonna be late Mick. I don't want you gettin' the sack an' spendin' your days idlin' round like our Sammy. Come on.

MICKEY *instead of making an effort to go, stands looking at her.*

MICKEY: Mam!

MRS JOHNSTONE: What?

MICKEY: What!

MRS JOHNSTONE: Come on.

MICKEY: Mam. Linda's pregnant!
A moment.

MRS JOHNSTONE: Do you love her?

MICKEY: Yeh!

MRS JOHNSTONE: When's the weddin'?

MICKEY: We thought, about a month . . . before Christmas anyway. Mam, could we live here for a bit?
She looks at him and nods.
Are you mad?

MRS JOHNSTONE: At you? Some hypocrite I'd be. No . . . I'm not mad son. I'm just thinkin' . . . you've not had much of a life with me, have y'?

MICKEY: Don't be stupid, course I have. You're great, you are, Mam. (*He gives her a quick kiss.*) Tar-ra I'd better get a move on. They've started layin' people off in the other factory y' know. Tarrah, Mam. Thanks.
MICKEY *exits.*

Music.

MRS JOHNSTONE *watches him go. As 'Miss Jones' begins she whips off her overall and a wedding suit is underneath. She acquires a hat.*

A wedding party assembles. MICKEY *remains in his working clothes.* LINDA *is in white. Other guests are suitably attired.*

A MANAGING DIRECTOR *enters and sings as his secretary,* MISS JONES, *takes notes.*

MR LYONS (*singing*): Take a letter, Miss Jones (quote)
I regret to inform you,
That owing to circumstances
Quite beyond our control.
It's a premature retirement
For those surplus to requirement,
I'm afraid it's a sign of the times,
Miss Jones,
An unfortunate sign of the times.

Throughout the next verse we see the wedding party wave goodbye to MICKEY *who goes to work, only to have his cards given to him when he gets there.*

Take a letter, Miss Jones,
Due to the world situation
The shrinking pound, the global slump,
And the price of oil
I'm afraid we must fire you,
We no longer require you,
It's just another
Sign of the times,
Miss Jones,
A most miserable sign of the times.

The GUESTS *at the wedding become a line of men looking for work.* MICKEY *joins them as* LINDA *watches. They are constantly met with shaking heads and by the end of the following verse have assembled in the dole office.*

Take a letter Miss Jones, of course we'll
Let the workforce know when
Inflation's been defeated
And recession is no more.
And for the moment we suggest
You don't become too depressed
As it's only a sign
Of the times,
Miss Jones,
A peculiar sign of the times.

Take a letter Miss Jones:
My dear Miss Jones, we'd like to thank you
Many years of splendid service,
Etcetara blah blah blah
You've been a perfect poppet
Yes that's right Miss Jones, you've got it
It's just another sign
Of the times,
Miss Jones, it's
Just another sign of the times.

He shows her the door. Crying she approaches the dole queue but then hesitates. The men in the queue take up the song.

DOLEITES: Dry your eyes, Miss Jones
It's not as bad as it seems (you)
Get used to being idle
In a year or two.
Unemployment's such a pleasure
These days, we call it leisure
It's just another sign
Of the times,
Miss Jones, it's
Just another sign of the times.

MICKEY *leaves the group and stands apart.* MISS JONES *takes his place. Behind* MICKEY *we can see* LINDA *and his* MOTHER.

There's a young man on the street, Miss Jones,
He's walkin' round in circles,
He's old before his time,
But still too young to know.
Don't look at him, don't cry though
This living on the Giro
Is only a sign of the times,
Miss Jones, it's
Just another sign of the times.
As they exit.
Miss Jones,
It's just another sign of the times . . .

CROWD *exits.*

MICKEY *is left alone, sitting dejected. We hear Christmas Bells.*

EDWARD *enters in a duffle coat and college scarf, unseen by* MICKEY. EDWARD *creeps up behind* MICKEY *and puts his hands over his eyes.*

EDWARD: Guess who?

MICKEY: Father Christmas.

EDWARD (*leaping out in front of them*): Mickey . . . (*Laughing.*) Merry Christmas.

MICKEY, unamused, looks at EDWARD and then looks away.

Come on then . . . I'm back, where's the action, the booze, the Christmas parties, the music and the birds.

No reaction.

What's wrong, Mickey?

MICKEY: Nothin'. How's University?

EDWARD: Mickey, it's fantastic. I haven't been to so many parties in my life. And there's just so many tremendous people, but you'll meet them Mick, some of them, Baz, Ronnie and Clare and oh, lots of them. They're coming over to stay for the New Year, for the party. Ooh it's just . . . it's great, Mickey.

MICKEY: Good.

EDWARD: Come on, what's wrong? It's nearly Christmas, we were going to do everything. How's Linda?

MICKEY: She's OK.

EDWARD (*trying again to rally him*): Well, come on then, let's go then . . . come on.

MICKEY: Come on where?

EDWARD: Mickey, what's wrong?

MICKEY: You. You're a dick head!

EDWARD is slightly unsure but laughs anyway.

There are no parties arranged. There is no booze or music. Christmas? I'm sick to the teeth of Christmas an' it isn't even here yet. See, there's very little to celebrate, Eddie. Since you left I've been walking around all day, every day, lookin' for a job.

EDWARD: What about the job you had?

MICKEY: It disappeared. (*Pause.*) Y' know somethin', I bleedin' hated that job, standin' there all day never doin' nothin' but put cardboard boxes together. I used to get . . . used to get terrified that I'd have to do it for the rest of me life. But, but after three months of nothin', the same answer everywhere, nothin', nothin' down for y', I'd crawl back to that job for half the pay and double the hours. Just . . . just makin' up boxes it was. But after bein' fucked off from everywhere, it seems like it was paradise.

Pause.

EDWARD: Why . . . why is a job so important? If I couldn't get a job I'd just say, sod it and draw the dole, live like a bohemian, tilt my hat to the world and say 'screw you'. So you're not working. Why is it so important?

MICKEY (*looking at him*): You don't understand anythin' do y'? I don't wear a hat that I could tilt at the world.

EDWARD: Look . . . come on . . . I've got money, plenty of it. I'm back, let's forget about bloody jobs, let's go and get Linda and celebrate. Look, look, money, lots of it, have some . . . (*He tries to thrust some notes into* MICKEY*'s hands.*)

MICKEY: No. I don't want your money, stuff it.

He throws the notes to the ground. EDWARD *picks them up and stands looking at* MICKEY.

Eddie, just do me a favour an' piss off, will y'?

Pause.

EDWARD: I thought, I thought we always stuck together. I thought we were . . . were blood brothers.

MICKEY: That was kids' stuff, Eddie. Didn't anyone tell y'? (*He looks at* EDWARD.) But I suppose you still are a kid, aren't y'?

EDWARD: I'm exactly the same age as you, Mickey.

MICKEY: Yeh. But you're still a kid. An' I wish I could be as well Eddie, I wish I could still believe in all that blood brother stuff. But I can't, because while no one was looking I grew up. An' you didn't, because you didn't need to; an' I don't blame y' for it Eddie. In your shoes I'd be the same, I'd still be able to be a kid. But I'm not in your shoes, I'm in these, lookin' at you. An' you make me sick, right? That was all just kids' stuff, Eddie, an' I don't want to be reminded of it. Right? So just, just take yourself away. Go an' see your friends an' celebrate with them.

Pause.

Go on . . . beat it before I hit y'.

EDWARD *looks at* MICKEY *and then slowly backs away.*

SAMMY *approaches* MICKEY *as, on the other side, we see* LINDA *hurrying on passing* EDWARD *who stops and calls.*

EDWARD: Linda!

SAMMY: Mickey.

EDWARD: Linda.

Reluctantly she stops, goes back a few paces.

Hello, Linda.

LINDA: Hello, Eddie.

EDWARD: Why haven't you called to see me?

LINDA: I heard you had friends, I didn't like butting in.

EDWARD: You'd never be butting in and you know it. It wouldn't matter if I never saw those friends again, if I could be with you.

LINDA: Eddie . . .

SAMMY: Look, I'm offerin' . . . all we need is someone to keep the eye for us. Look at y' Mickey. What have y' got? Nothin', like me Mam. Where y' takin' y' tart for New Year? Nowhere.

EDWARD: You might as well know, if I'm not going to, see you again. I've always loved you, you must have known that.

SAMMY: We don't *use* the shooters. They're just frighteners. Y' don' need to use them. Everyone behaves when they see a shooter. You won't even be where the action is. Just keep the eye out for us.

EDWARD: I'm sorry.

SAMMY: Fifty quid Mickey. Fifty quid for an hour's work. Just think where y' could take Linda if you had cash like that.

EDWARD: I'm sorry, Linda.

LINDA: It's all right. I suppose, I suppose I always . . . loved you, in a way.

EDWARD: Then marry me.

LINDA: Didn't Mickey tell y'? We got married two weeks before you came home and I'm expecting a baby.

MICKEY: Fifty notes?

SAMMY *nods.*

All right.

SAMMY: Great.

MICKEY *nods.*

Cheer up, will y'? It's New Year.

SAMMY *exits.*

EDWARD'S FRIENDS (*variously; off*): Where's Lyo? Come on Lyons, you pillock, you're supposed to be helping us with the booze. Come on Lyonese. Edward, come on.

LINDA: I'll see y' Eddie. Happy New Year. (*She moves away.*)

EDWARD *exits.*

MICKEY: Linda . . . Linda . . .

LINDA: Are you comin' in?

MICKEY: Look . . . I'll be back about eight o'clock. An' listen, get dressed up. I'm takin' y' out.

LINDA: What?

MICKEY: We're goin' dancin'. Right? Then we're goin' for a slap-up meal an' tomorrow you can go into town an' get some new clothes.

LINDA: Oh yeh? Where's the money comin' from?

MICKEY: I'm . . . doin' some work . . .

LINDA: What?

MICKEY: Look, stop arguin', will y'? I'm doin' some work and then I'm takin' you out.

SAMMY (*off*): Mickey!

LINDA: Is that your Sammy?

MICKEY: Now shut up, Linda. Right, right? Just make sure you're ready at eight . . . (*He starts to leave.*)

LINDA (*as he goes*): Mickey . . . Mickey . . . No!

LINDA *exits.*
MICKEY *moves away.*

The NARRATOR *enters.*
SAMMY *enters.*

NARRATOR: There's a full moon shining and a joker in the pack,
The dealers dealt the cards, and he won't take them back,
There's a black cat stalking and a woman who's afraid,
That there's no getting off without the price being paid.

We see MICKEY, *nervously keeping look-out as behind him, as if inside a filling station office, we see* SAMMY, *his back to us, talking to an off-stage character.*

SAMMY: Don't piss about with me, pal . . . I said give! (*Pause.*) Listen, it's not a toy y' know . . . We're not playin' games. Y' don't get up again if one of these hits y' . . . What are you doin'? I said listen to me, I said . . . don't you fuckin' touch that . . . Listen.

An alarm bell is heard, followed by an explosion from the gun. SAMMY *reels backwards. He and* MICKEY *run and enter their house.*

NARRATOR: There's a man lies bleeding on a garage floor,
SAMMY: Quick, get in the house an' bolt the fuckin' door.

MICKEY *stands unable to move, tears streaming down his face.*

NARRATOR: And maybe, if you counted ten and kept your
fingers crossed

It would all be just a game and then no one would have lost.

MICKEY: You shot him, you shot him.

SAMMY: I know I bloody did.

MICKEY: You shot him, you shot him.

SAMMY: Move, I've got to get this hid.

LINDA (*off*): Mickey . . . Mickey, is that you?

SAMMY: Ooh, fuck . . . (*He quickly pulls back a mat, pulls up a floorboard and puts the gun beneath it.*)

LINDA *enters.*

Two POLICEMEN *arrive at the house.*

SAMMY *splits out the back.* MICKEY *remains silently crying.* LINDA *goes to him and puts her arms around him. As* SAMMY *is being apprehended at the back, the other* POLICEMAN *enters and gently removes* LINDA *from* MICKEY *and leads him out and into the police station.*

LINDA: But I've ironed him a shirt.

Music.

MICKEY, *placed in a prison cell, stands quietly crying.* MRS JOHNSTON *enters.*

MRS JOHNSTONE (*singing*): The jury found him guilty
Sent him down for seven years,
Though he acted like they gave him life,
He couldn't stop the tears.
And when we went to visit him,
He didn't want to know,
It seems like jail's sent him off the rails,
Just like Marilyn Monroe
His mind's gone dancing
Can't stop dancing

A DOCTOR *enters the cell and examines* MICKEY.

They showed him to a doctor,
And after routine test,
A prescription note the doctor wrote,
For the chronically depressed.
And now the tears have stopped
He sits and counts the days to go
And treats his ills with daily pills
Just like Marilyn Monroe.

The DOCTOR *exits.*

They stop his mind from dancing
Stop it dancing.

A prison warder leads LINDA *into the cell. He indicates a seat opposite* MICKEY.

LINDA: What are y' doin'?

MICKEY: What? I'm takin' me tablet.

LINDA: Listen, Mickey. I've told y'. They're just junk. You'll be home soon, Mickey, and you should come off them.

MICKEY: Why? I need . . . I need to take them.

LINDA: Listen, Mickey, you've . . .

MICKEY: No! See, he says, the doctor, he said . . .

LINDA: What did he say?

MICKEY: He said, about me nerves. An' how I get depressed an' I need to take these cos they make me better . . .

LINDA: I get depressed but I don't take those. You don't need those, Mickey.

MICKEY: Leave me alone, will y'? I can't cope with this. I'm not well. The doctor said, didn't he, I'm not well . . . I can't do things . . . leave me alone . . .

The WARDER *escorts* LINDA *from the cell.*

Throughout the following verse MICKEY *leaves the prison and goes home.*

MRS JOHNSTONE (*singing*): With grace for good behaviour
He got out before his time
The family and the neighbours told him
He was lookin' fine.
But he's feelin' fifteen years older
And his speech is rather slow
And the neighbours said
You'd think he was dead
Like Marilyn Monroe
No cause for dancing
No more dancing . . .

LINDA *approaches* MRS JOHNSTONE. LINDA *is weighed down with shopping bags and is weary.*

MRS JOHNSTONE: Linda, where've y' been? We've gorra do somethin' about him. He's been out for months and he's still takin' those pills. Linda, he needs a job, you two need a place of your own an' . . .

LINDA: Mam . . . Mam that's why I'm late, I've been to see . . . We're movin' at the end of the month. We've got our own place an' I think I've got Mickey a job . . .

MRS JOHNSTONE: Oh, Jesus, thank God. But how . . .

LINDA: It's all right . . . I . . someone I know . . .

MRS JOHNSTONE: But who . . .

LINDA: It's all right Mam. Did y' get our Sarah from school?

MRS JOHNSTONE: Yeh, she's in bed, but listen how did y' manage to . . .

LINDA: Never mind, Mam. Mam, isn't it great; if he's workin' an' we've got our own place he'll be able to get himself together an' stop takin' those friggin' things . . .

They start to leave.

MRS JOHNSTONE: But, listen Linda, who . . .

LINDA: Oh just some . . . some feller I know. He's . . . he's on the housin' committee. You don't know him, Mam . . .

MRS JOHNSTONE *exits.*

MICKEY *and* LINDA *are in their new house. In the lounge* LINDA *is preparing* MICKEY*'s working things.*

(*Shouting*): Mickey, Mickey, come on, you'll be late . . .

MICKEY *enters his house.*

MICKEY: Where's me . . .

LINDA: Here . . . here's y' bag. Y' sandwiches are in there . . .

He ignores the bag and begins looking through a cupboard drawer.

Mickey, what y' lookin' for?

MICKEY: Y' know what I'm lookin' for.

LINDA: Mickey, Mickey listen to me . . .

MICKEY: Where's me tablets gone, Linda?

LINDA: Mickey you don't need your tablets!

MICKEY: Linda!

LINDA: Mickey. You're workin' now, we're livin' on our own – you've got to start makin' an effort.

MICKEY: Give them to me, Linda.

LINDA: You promised.

MICKEY: I know I promised but I can't do without them. I tried. Last week I tried to do without them. By dinner time I was shakin' an' sweating so much I couldn't even work. I need them. That's all there is to it. Now give.

Pause.

LINDA: Is that it then? Are y' gonna stay on them forever?

MICKEY: Linda.

LINDA: Look. We've . . . we've managed to sort ourselves out this far but what's the use if . . .

MICKEY: *We* have sorted ourselves out? Do you think I'm really stupid?

LINDA: What?

MICKEY: I didn't sort anythin' out Linda. Not a job, not a house, nothin'. It used to be just sweets an' ciggies he gave me, because I had none of me own. Now it's a job and a house. I'm not stupid, Linda. You sorted it out. You an' Councillor Eddie Lyons.

LINDA *doesn't deny it.*

Now give me the tablets . . . I need them.

LINDA: An' what about what I need? I need you. I love you. But, Mickey, not when you've got them inside you. When you take those things, Mickey, I can't even see you.

MICKEY: That's why I take them. So I can be invisible. (*Pause.*) Now give me them.

Music. We see LINDA *mutely hand* MICKEY *her bag.*
MICKEY *quickly grabs the tablets.*
MICKEY *exits.*

The NARRATOR *enters.*

The NARRATOR *watches* LINDA. *She moves to telephone, but hesitates.*

NARRATOR: There's a girl inside the woman
Who's waiting to get free
She's washed a million dishes
She's always making tea.

LINDA (*speaking on the 'phone*): Could I talk to Councillor Lyons, please?

NARRATOR: There's a girl inside the woman
And the mother she became
And a half remembered song
Comes to her lips again.

LINDA (*on the 'phone*): Eddie, could I talk to you? Yeh, I remember.

NARRATOR: The girl would sing the melody
But the woman stands in doubt
And wonders what the price would be
For letting the young girl out.

MRS JOHNSTONE *enters.*

MRS JOHNSTONE (*singing*): It's just a light romance,
It's nothing cruel,
They laid no plans,

How it came,
Who can explain?

LINDA *approaches* EDWARD *who is waiting at the park fence.*

They just said 'hello',
And foolishly they gazed,
They should have gone
Their separate ways.

The music continues.

EDWARD: Hey. (*He mimes firing a gun.*)

LINDA: Missed.

EDWARD *laughs, grabbing* LINDA *jokingly. Their smiles fade as they look at each other. Suddenly they kiss. They walk together, hand in hand. All this through the following verse.*

MRS JOHNSTONE (*singing*): It's just the same old song,
Nothing cruel,
Nothing wrong.
It's just two fools,
Who know the rules,
But break them all,
And grasp at half a chance
To play their part
In a light romance.

Throughout the following chorus we see MICKEY *at work. We see him go to take his pills. We see him make the effort of not taking them. We see the strain of this upon him but see that he is determined.*

Living on the never never,
Constant as the changing weather,
Never sure
Who's at the door,
Or the price
You're gonna have to pay.

We see LINDA *and* EDWARD *kicking up the leaves before parting.*

It's just a secret glance,
Across a room.
A touch of hands
That part too soon.
That same old tune
That always plays,
And lets them dance as friends,

Then stand apart,
As the music ends.

During the next chorus EDWARD *and* LINDA *wave goodbye, as* EDWARD *and* MICKEY *once did.*

MRS LYONS *enters and goes to* MICKEY.

She turns MICKEY *round and points out* EDWARD *and* LINDA *to him. By the end of the chorus* MICKEY *is hammering on his own door.*

Living on the never never,
Constant as the changing weather,
Never sure
Who's at the door
Or the price you're gonna have to pay.

As the music abruptly segues MICKEY *is heard hammering on his door and calling for* LINDA, *as he once did for his mother. The music pulsates and builds as he runs to his mothers's house. He enters and flings back the floorboard to reveal the gun hidden by* SAMMY.

MRS JOHNSTONE *enters just as* MICKEY *disappears with the gun.*

MRS JOHNSTONE (*screaming*): Mickey . . . Mickey . . .

We see MICKEY *comb the town, breaking through groups of people, looking, searching, desperate, not even knowing what he's looking for or what he is going to do. His mother is frantically trying to catch him but not succeeding.*

NARRATOR: There's a man gone mad in the town tonight,
He's gonna shoot somebody down,
There's a man gone mad, lost his mind tonight
There's a mad man
There's a mad man
There's a mad man running round and round.

Now you know the devil's got your number,
He's runnin' right beside you,
He's screamin' deep inside you,
And someone said he's callin' your number up today.

As MRS JOHNSTONE *makes her way to* LINDA*'s house.*

There's a mad man/There's a mad man/There's a mad man.

MRS JOHNSTONE *hammers on* LINDA*'s door, shouting her name.* LINDA, *just returning home, comes up behind her.*

LINDA: Mam . . . Mam . . . what's . . .

MRS JOHNSTONE (*out of breath*) He's . . . Mickey . . . Mickey's got a gun . . .

LINDA: Mickey? . . . Eddie? . . . The Town Hall . . .

MRS JOHNSTONE: What?

LINDA (*beginning to run*): Eddie Lyons!

NARRATOR: There's a mad man running round and round
You know the devil's got your number
You know he's right beside you
He's screamin' deep inside you
And someone said he's callin' your number up today
Today
Today
TODAY!

On the last three words of the chorus MRS JOHNSON *runs off. On the last 'Today' the music stops abruptly.*

We see EDWARD, *standing behind a table, on a platform. He is in the middle of addressing his audience. Two Councillors stand either side.*

EDWARD: And if, for once, I agree with Councillor Smith, you mustn't hold that against me. But in this particular instance, yes, I do agree with him. You're right, Bob, there is a light at the end of the tunnel. Quite right. None of us would argue with you on that score. But what we would question is this, how many of us . . .

From his audience a commotion beginning. He thinks he is being heckled and so tries to carry on. In fact his audience is reacting to the sight of MICKEY *appearing from the stalls, a gun held two-handed, to steady his shaking hands, and pointed directly at* EDWARD. EDWARD *turns and sees* MICKEY *as someone on the platform next to him realizes the reality of the situation and screams.*

MICKEY: Stay where you are!

MICKY *stops a couple of yards from* EDWARD. *He is unsteady and breathing awkwardly.*

EDWARD (*eventually*): Hello, Mickey.

MICKEY: I stopped takin' the pills.

EDWARD (*pause*): Oh.

MICKEY (*eventually*): I began thinkin' again. Y' see. (*To the* COUNCILLOR.) Just get her out of here, mister, now!

The COUNCILLORS *hurry off.*

EDWARD *and* MICKEY *are now alone on the platform.*

I had to start thinkin' again. Because there was one thing left in my life. (*Pause.*) Just one thing I had left, Eddie – Linda –

an' I wanted to keep her. So, so I stopped takin' the pills. But it was too late. D' y' know who told me about . . . you . . . an' Linda . . . Your mother . . . she came to the factory and told me.

EDWARD: Mickey, I don't know what she told you but Linda and I are just friends . . .

MICKEY (*shouting for the first time*): Friends! I could kill you. We were friends weren't we? Blood brothers, wasn't it? Remember?

EDWARD: Yes, Mickey, I remember.

MICKEY: Well, how come you got everything . . . an' I got nothin'? (*Pause.*) Friends. I've been thinkin' again Eddie. You an' Linda were friends when she first got pregnant, weren't y'?

EDWARD: Mickey!

MICKEY: Does my child belong to you as well as everythin' else? Does she, Eddie, does she?

EDWARD (*shouting*): No, for God's sake!

Pause.

From the back of the auditorium we hear a POLICEMAN *through a loudhailer.*

POLICEMAN 1: Now listen, son, listen to me; I've got armed marksmen with me. But if you do exactly as I say we won't need to use them, will we? Now look, Michael, put down the gun, just put the gun down, son.

MICKEY (*dismissing their presence*): What am I doin' here Eddie? I thought I was gonna shoot y'. But I can't even do that. I don't even know if the thing's loaded.

MRS JOHNSTONE *slowly walks down the centre aisle towards the platform.*

POLICEMAN 2: What's that woman doin'?

POLICEMAN 1: Get that woman away . . .

POLICEMAN 2: Oh Christ.

MRS JOHNSTONE: Mickey. Mickey. Don't shoot him Mickey . . .

MICKEY *continues to hold the gun in position.*

MICKEY: Go away Mam . . . Mam you go away from here.

MRS JOHNSTONE: No, son. (*She walks on to the platform.*)

MICKEY (*shouting*): Mam!

MRS JOHNSTONE: Mickey. Don't shoot Eddie. He's your brother. You had a twin brother. I couldn't afford to keep both of you. His mother couldn't have kids. I agreed to give one of you away!

MICKEY (*something that begins deep down inside him*): You! (*Screaming.*) You! Why didn't you give me away! (*He stands glaring at her, almost uncontrollable with rage.*) I could have been . . . I could have been him!

On the word 'him' MICKEY *waves at* EDWARD *with his gun hand. The gun explodes and blows* EDWARD *apart.* MICKEY *turns to the* POLICE *screaming the word 'No'. They open fire and four guns explode, blowing* MICKEY *away.*

LINDA *runs down the aisle.*

The POLICE *are heard through the loudhailer.*

Nobody move, please. It's all right, it's all over, just stay where you are.

Music.

As the Light on the scene begins to dim we see the NARRATOR, *watching.*

NARRATOR: And do we blame superstition for what came to pass?
Or could it be what we, the English, have come to know as class?
Did you ever hear the story of the Johnstone twins,
As like each other as two new pins,
How one was kept and one given away,
How they were born, and they died, on the self same day?

MRS JOHNSTONE (*singing*): Tell me it's not true,
Say it's just a story.
Something on the news
Tell me it's not true.
Though it's here before me,
Say it's just a dream,
Say it's just a scene
From an old movie of years ago,
From an old movie of Marilyn Monroe.

Say it's just some clowns,
Two players in the limelight,
And bring the curtain down.
Say it's just two clowns,
Who couldn't get their lines right,
Say it's just a show
On the radio,
That we can turn over and start again,
That we can turn over; it's only a game.

COMPANY: Tell me it's not true,
Say I only dreamed it,
And morning will come soon,
Tell me it's not true,
Say you didn't mean it,
Say it's just pretend,
Say it's just the end,
Of an old movie from years ago
Of an old movie with Marilyn Monroe.

Curtain.

Teaching notes

What it's all about – meaning and plot

> So did y' hear the story of the Johnstone twins?
> As like each other as two new pins . . .

A good story has more than one meaning, or different levels of meaning, and this is true of *Blood Brothers*.

To start with, discuss the following statements with someone. Try to agree which statement sums up best what *Blood Brothers* is about and rank the rest of the statements in order of importance.

The play is

a) about how the class system in this country affects the life chances of the people who live here.
b) about the way mothers destroy their sons by loving them too much.
c) about life in Liverpool, a comedy that ends in tragedy.
d) about the contrast between a working-class woman and a rich woman.
e) about twins who are separated at birth and who suffer violent deaths on the same day when they are in their twenties.
f) a love story in which a woman who is trapped in a marriage to an ex-prisoner seeks fulfilment with a friend from the past.
g) about how superstition governs our lives.

Ideas for talking and writing

1. How many reasons can you find for using the word 'blood' in the title of the play.

2. 'The lights come up to show the re-enactment of the final

moments of the play – the deaths of Mickey and Edward. The scene fades.'

Does it take away interest from a story if you know how it ends? How much would an audience, seeing the play for the first time, grasp about what was going to happen?

3. Prepare about 250 words giving a synopsis of the play, making sure that the reader knows who the characters are and what happens to them. You must distinguish between important events and minor details. So, for example, you would need to say that Linda as a little girl tends to dominate the boys but you would not need to mention that she is the one who hits the target when they are firing the pellet gun in the park. That is a detail you might use when you are talking or writing about Linda.

Studying the characters

> Plays like *Shirley Valentine* and *Educating Rita* start with a character and the plot follows but with *Blood Brothers* the whole story was there and the characters had to be invented to inhabit the story. (Willy Russell)

Who is the most influential character in the play? Work with somebody to rank the following people in order of importance and justify your preferences:

> The Narrator, Mrs Johnstone, Mrs Lyons, Linda, Mickey, Eddie, Sammy, Mr Lyons

Whether you are preparing to play a character on stage or to write an essay about a character the process you have to go through is similar. You need to study the text and make notes as you go along. If you are going to give a talk on Linda and then use your notes to write a character study you might decide to divide your talk into six sections and prepare a prompt card for each section:

- her appearance
- her childhood and background

- her relationship with Mickey
- the way she tries to control her life
- the way her life is shaped by events outside her control
- her relationship with Eddie

Prompt card 1: Linda's appearance

We are not told what Linda looks like because the same actress has to play her looking like a little girl, as a teenager and as a mature woman.

Prompt card 2: Linda's childhood and background

We are not told anything about her parents or family.

p. 30 Linda is first mentioned. She and Mickey are in one gang, Sammy in another.

p. 32 She moves to protect Mickey.

p. 33 Linda is undaunted by Sammy.

p. 33 She seems much older than Mickey.

p. 34 She has a sense of humour. 'We try an' shoot his little thingy off.'

p. 36 She is a daredevil. 'Let's throw some stones through them windows.'

Prompt card 3: Linda's relationship with Mickey

p. 32 Linda moves in to protect Mickey who is visibly shaken.

p. 48 On the bus Linda protects Mickey from Sammy.

p. 52 Linda stands up for Mickey in the classroom. 'Take no notice Mickey. I love you.'

p. 54 Linda tries to get Mickey to kiss her. 'I give up with you, Mickey Johnstone. I'm off. You get on my bleedin' nerves.'

p. 66 Mickey asks Linda to go out with him. 'My God. Y' take y' time gettin' goin' but then there's no stoppin' y'.'

p. 67 Mickey: 'Mam. Linda's pregnant.'

p. 75 Linda visits Mickey in prison. 'Listen, Mickey. I've told y'. They're just junk. You'll be home soon, Mickey, and you should come off them.'

p. 75 'I think I've got Mickey a job.'

p. 77 Mickey and Linda are on stage together for the last

time. 'I need you. I love you. But, Mickey, not when you've got them inside you.'

Prompt card 4: Linda is in control

p. 31 She catches the grenade and lobs it back to the soldiers.
p. 36 She hits the target with the gun.
p. 36 She suggests they break the windows.
p. 50 She tells Mickey she loves him.
p. 75 She gets them rehoused and gets Mickey a job.
p. 77 She telephones Eddie and starts the relationship that will end in death.

Prompt card 5: Linda is controlled by events

p. 67 She becomes pregnant.
p. 67 They can't afford a house of their own.
p. 68 Mickey is made redundant.
p. 74 Mickey is sent to prison.
p. 79 Mrs Lyons tells Mickey about Linda and Eddie.

Prompt card 6: Linda's relationship with Eddie

p. 36 She dominates him in the gang. 'He is look. Eddie's scared.'
p. 54 They meet as teenagers. She tries to wind Mickey up by saying 'He's gorgeous, isn't he?'
p. 56 Edward: 'Wow, was that Linda? And is she your girl friend?'
p. 62 The three of them are having a great time. Narrator: 'There's a few bob in your pocket and you've got good friends.'
p. 65 Edward: 'He's mad. If I was Mickey I would have asked you years ago.'
p. 72 Edward: 'I've always loved you, you must have known that.' Linda: 'I suppose I always . . . loved you, in a way.'
p. 78 'Their smiles fade as they look at each other. Suddenly they kiss.'

When you give your talk or write your character study you should use a mixture of direct quotations, references to events, and references to stage directions so that they fit smoothly into what you say or write. For example:

> As Sammy is trying to persuade Mickey to take part in the robbery, Eddie and Linda meet. He does not know that Linda and Mickey are married so, thinking that they will not meet again, Eddie confesses: 'I've always loved you, you must have known that,' and Linda haltingly admits: 'I suppose. I suppose I always . . . loved you, in a way.' Several years later, after Mickey has been in prison and Linda realises she cannot break him of his dependence on tranquillisers, she telephones Eddie. The stage directions tell us: 'Edward laughs, grabbing Linda jokingly. Their smiles fade as they look at each other. Suddenly they kiss. They walk together hand in hand.' As they walk away Mrs Johnstone sings, 'It's just two fools, who know the rules, but break them all, and grasp at half a chance to play their part in a light romance.'

The actors speak

Sympathetic but detached

When Andrew Schofield was at school in Liverpool he was selected to play a Scouse lad in Willy Russell's *Death of a Young Young Man*. Eight years later, already with a well-established acting career, he auditioned to play the guitar in *Blood Brothers* in the first production at the Liverpool Playhouse.

> I didn't pass the audition for that but I was offered the part of the Narrator. I have a feeling Willy wanted me for it. To be honest, at first I thought the play a bit sentimental. I wasn't bothered that it was too obviously political or was stating the obvious about class in Britain but I just thought it was sentimental. And then at the first run-through I found myself sitting there actually crying at the scene where Eddie gives Mickey a present because he's going away. I did something similar when I was a kid and we moved away and it brought it all back to me. That's the

point about Willy. He writes about things that have actually happened to people. I don't mean everyone has had twins and given one away but we've all experienced, directly or indirectly, the hardship that Mrs Johnstone goes through. It's a powerful and simple thing: your life is determined by the class you are in. And it's even more true now than it was when he wrote it. You test the kids so that the majority fail and then you filter out a few from the ones who pass.

I was the first Narrator so in that sense I created the part but in reality it was all there. I just followed my instinct. At the first run-through I was sitting next to the director, Chris Bond, and when we came to the Milkman he said, 'You read that', and the same with the Judge and the Teacher. I don't know whether Willy had meant it to be like that but I suppose Chris had it all worked out. I was on stage most of the time except when I went off to change for one of the other parts. I've only seen the play once since then but I understand the role of the Narrator has been simplified. When I prepare a part I do a lot of note-taking and reading but I don't like to waffle and I try to keep it simple. So I saw the Narrator as one of the old story-tellers, a bit like the Greek chorus. I don't see him as a sinister person. He's not cruel or sly, not like Mephistopheles. But he does have knowledge. He is not the controller of events but he is able to say, 'Here's what happens next' or 'Watch what happens next'. I saw him as being sympathetic but detached.

I loved the part. I did eight weeks in Liverpool and then three months in the West End. We had a great cast and we slipped in and out of the parts easily. There was no problem about playing the part of kids. We all had a great time in rehearsal remembering the games we used to play and incorporating them into the songs. I left the production because I wouldn't have done it justice if I'd stayed any longer. People would have been paying money to see me looking bored and I know, once that happens, it's no good.

I think it's a great play for kids to study. They can relate to it immediately. What teenager doesn't understand the friendship of the boys, the mother's plight, the first kiss, the temptation of crime, the unexpected pregnancy, the young woman trapped in a marriage and the lure of romantic love even though it threatens a relationship?

Just two women, one can have children, one can't

Stephanie Lawrence has played Mrs Johnstone at the Phoenix Theatre and on Broadway, six days a week for four years with scarcely a break. Joanna Monroe has been in *Blood Brothers* twice, as both Mrs Johnstone and Mrs Lyons. She has played Mrs Lyons and understudied for Mrs Johnstone simultaneously. It has not been unknown for her to play one part in the afternoon and the other part in the evening.

Joanna: The difference between the two mothers is very real but they have a common bond which is that they both love children. That is terribly important. People tend to think of Mrs Lyons as being a 'baddie' but she is not. She is a person who makes a big mistake because she loves children. She is desperate for a baby and she thinks by helping out this woman who has too many children she is doing the right thing. She thinks she will be providing herself and her husband who cannot have children with something which is going to make their marriage happier and richer. She is going to give a child a wonderful home and she does it for what she considers to be the best reasons. But, as we know, it turns out wrong because jealousy and guilt rear their ugly heads. Mrs Lyons is not vicious. She is desperate. The way I approach the part is through love. I think you have to do that.

Stephanie: You also have to give the audience a problem. I don't think you can say Mrs Johnstone is all good and Mrs Lyons is all bad. If you do that it becomes like a panto and you've got the audience hissing and cheering.

Joanna: The point is Mrs Lyons is a woman who worships her husband, adores him and is desperate to give him a child. She does this by wrongly taking a child and loving that child beyond reason. Any mother will tell you. You would kill for your child. It does turn Mrs Lyons mad and she does go for Mrs Johnstone with a knife, but it is not a calculated move.

Stephanie: I think that's what the equaliser is between the two mothers. They would both kill for their kids. They are side by side, both mothers. When Mrs Lyons goes for the knife she thinks she is protecting her son from finding out the truth. It is not a calculated move. She doesn't go to the house to kill her. In fact she doesn't know what she will find there. All she sees is the boys coming from a house and she thinks, 'This is the end. My child is going to be taken from me.'

Joanna: It's at that moment she goes off the wall but I don't play her as a mad woman. I play her as distraught and I try to portray the pain. The madness comes out of jealousy and grief and pain. Anyone who has lost anybody or has been in this kind of emotional situation knows this terrifying madness. Sanity goes and what is left is grief and passion. Jealousy is the most corrupting of all emotions. It can poison every thought and every moment. Every time I play the part the emotion hits me and every time it comes as a surprise because when we hit that scene we never know what's going to happen.

Stephanie: You see we know each other so well and we work together so well we can go to a scene like that without quite knowing where it's going to go. So every night it's different.

Joanna: The last scene when she betrays the secret is the awful thing. Every night, when Mickey turns back and I look into his eyes it makes me feel: 'What have I done?'

Stephanie: Why does she do it?

Joanna: It's the jealousy. She wants to break those boys up so that she can break the bond, so that she can have her sons back. In order to do that she has to prove to Mickey that Eddie is no friend. 'Look at what he is doing with your wife.'

Stephanie: I've played Mrs Johnstone here and in the States and the reception is always the same. As long as we are doing a good show we get a standing ovation. I believe in the class implications of this play because I grew up in and around the working class. I don't entirely believe that your status in life depends on the class you're born into. What is more important is the effect of grinding poverty. But even that doesn't mean you cannot become something special. Mrs Johnstone was trapped because of her children. Her husband had walked out on her and she loved them and had to look after them. If it was me I don't think I would be so trapped. I can put myself in her shoes but with me it wouldn't be so grey. I don't think she's a weak woman. She's a strong woman who puts her children before herself. She's a 'glad-and-sorry' mother. My parents came up the same way. My mother used to have the bailiffs at the front door and my father would be running out the back door. She used to call it glad-and-sorry: glad I've got it, sorry I have to pay for it. Of course, things got paid for in the end, but week-by-week. There is a lot of wishing in this play.

Joanna: And it's interesting it comes from both sides. We see the working-class mother working for the middle-class mother and that is very quickly got rid of, the balance changes. As far as I am concerned, at the start of Act Two Mrs Johnstone is the person who is rich and has strength. She is the one who can stand there and say, 'Yes, I've achieved this through honesty and hard work.' She has this great love around her whereas Mrs Lyons has nothing except this terrible burden. Mrs Johnstone has a richness of spirit that Mrs Lyons craves. But the wishes come from both sides.

Stephanie: Mrs Johnstone is a character who bounces back. She's had so many knocks there is not much left you can sling at her. She has the money in her hand and she throws it away. She's not a sad character. She's a fighter and a winner. Think about it. She has a son who kills a man in an armed robbery and we don't know what happens to him. She has another son who does time for armed robbery and another son who turns out to be a successful politician. And both of those two end up dead in front of her. But who knows, she might meet somebody absolutely terrific and her life could change completely.

Joanna: I am exceedingly glad I don't have to play Mrs

Lyons as it was in the original play where she does the killing. In this one we have two bodies and three women grieving over the dead brothers.

Stephanie: Yes Eddie goes off to university and becomes a councillor but what does he want out of life? He loses the one person he loves, Linda. He gives her to Mickey. Mickey has everything Eddie wants and Eddie has everything Mickey wants. It's the same with the mothers.

Joanna: Willy Russell writes beautifully for women. And yet he once apologised to me because he felt he hadn't done Mrs Lyons justice. He said he hadn't enjoyed writing about her when she was successful and rich. I believe it's when Mrs Lyons is falling apart that he enjoys the writing. I think that's why it's such a challenge.

Stephanie: It's got to be the hardest part in the show to play it well.

Joanna: It's a swine.

Stephanie: I've got the songs and my part is straightforward, black and white.

Joanna: It is a nightmare. I don't want to do Mrs Lyons a disservice by standing there and making out she is the Wicked Witch of the West.

Stephanie: There has to be sympathy for both of them.

Joanna: I never forget when I first did this with Steph in 1990 I was called to the stage door and outside there was this family with a little five-year-old weeping her eyes out. I said, 'Did I frighten you?' and she sobbed out, 'No it wasn't your fault you couldn't have a baby. You mustn't think they died because of you.' That's when it works. That means more to me than all the critics. But it is a burden carrying this part.

Stephanie: We mustn't forget the other woman in the play, Linda. In the text, when Mickey says he can't give up the tranquillisers, Eddie is the person she turns to for help both for herself and Mickey. He is the only person who knows them both equally. I don't for a moment believe she goes to Eddie out of want of love for herself.

Joanna: I've never felt that. She goes to him for help for both of them. I think her love for Mickey is so strong that I don't think there is a betrayal. Obviously there is an attraction but there is no betrayal. I don't believe for one minute that Linda and Eddie made love. And that is the tragedy. If Mrs Lyons hadn't told Mickey about what she had seen I think Eddie would have taken Linda in his arms and said, 'It's all right. We'll make this work. You go back home and I'll come round later with a bottle of wine and we'll just sit down and talk.' But everyone can have their own views on it. That's what makes it so interesting.

Stephanie: Just like the brothers, the bond between the two mothers has to be strong. Emotionally they are the same. At the end, you take all their clothes off and they are just two women. They each have a womb. One can have children and one can't.

Joanna: It's as simple as that. It's about being a woman and that longing for a child. That's what I love about working with Steph. We almost have silent communication.

Stephanie: We both have very long but very different journeys in this play. We finish up miles away from where we started and I find that emotionally exhausting. You also become very attached to your songs.

Joanna: Once this show is in your blood it never goes.

Working at the words

Dear Chris,
Here's Act One. Sorry you haven't the advantage of knowing the recently added melodies. Of course it's a hell of a long act (38 pages and a lot of music) but I'm not worried about that because the story is strong and fun, the pace and structure are there and should, therefore, provide a solid base from which to cut it.

But: where do I go from here? It's something I feel I have to finish because I could not bear the idea of having to put such a good first act onto the shelf; equally though (perhaps more so) I would not want to give an audience this first act and then disappoint them with a poor second. I think that the schemata of the second part of the original version contains little that is of use. It's a scheme rather than a story. I'm worried that events are arbitrary rather than inevitable/homogeneous/organic. I have good individual scenes for Act Two but scenes maketh not a story. The problem is that whereas in Act One we see the inevitable consequences of certain actions, my work on Act Two has been a misguided attempt at cobbling scenes with some vague result in mind. The scenes fail to point to the next inevitable consequence. Peggy Ramsay called me and asked me the crucial question: 'What's it about? What, put at its simplest, are you trying to say?' I answered: 'That class splits these two brothers, that class keeps them apart, that class killed them.' But I don't want to tell the audience that. I want the audience to watch the story and know why they were killed. (Extract from a letter written by Willy Russell to Chris Bond, director of the first production of *Blood Brothers*)

Comparison of two endings

Compare the ending of the original play without music and the ending of the final version.

Version 1: Original schools version without music

EDWARD: Look Mickey . . .

MICKEY: No! You look . . . 'cause I've got the power now. (*Waving the gun.*) This says I have. Move over there.

EDWARD *does so.*

Now move across there. (*He does so.*) Now over there . . . an' there . . . An' put y' hands up!

EDWARD: Don't you think you should put that thing away Mickey?

MICKEY (*shouting*): Don't you move! (*Pause.*) How does it feel Eddie? You're not in control now are y'? I am! (*Pause.*) I thought my job was mine; but it's not; you fixed it up. My house. It's not mine. You did it. My wife. Even Linda's not mine. My son, does he belong to you as well?

EDWARD: Mickey!

MICKEY: I should shoot you Eddie, do you know that. I

should shoot y'. But I know I won't. Because even with this . . . even holdin' this to your head, I'm still not in control of anythin' am I? I don't have any power do I?

EDWARD (*afraid*): I . . . I don't know Mickey.

MICKEY (*pause*): Don't y'? I do. It's not even a real gun Eddie! It's a model. A fake. Y' couldn't shoot nothin' with it. (*Holds it out as if to fire at* EDWARD.) Look!

The MOTHER *bursts into the scene. She screams at* MICKEY.

THE MOTHER: Mickey! Don't . . . Don't kill him!

MICKEY (*laughing*): It's alright, look it's just a . . . (*Going to fire.*)

THE MOTHER (*nodding*): Yes. You were twins.

The two of them looking at her.

MRS LYONS *enters with gun.*

MRS LYONS: You told them. I knew you would. You're a witch. But you see, it didn't come true. I'll still have Edward.

She goes to shoot MICKEY. EDWARD *screams 'Mother'. He runs in front of* MICKEY. EDWARD *is shot.* MRS LYONS *pauses a moment before turning the gun on* MICKEY. *They are both dead.*

NARRATOR: So did y' ever hear the tale of the
Johnstone twins,
As like each other as two new pins,
How one was kept, one given away,
They were born and they died on the self same day.

THE END

Version 2: Original script peformed at the Liverpool Playhouse

From his audience a commotion beginning. He thinks he is being heckled and so tries to carry on. In fact his audience is reacting to the sight of MICKEY *appearing from the stalls, a gun held two-handed to steady his shaking hands, and pointed directly at* EDWARD.

EDWARD: How many of us . . . eh? Question is . . .

He turns and sees MICKEY *as someone in the audience, realises it's for real and screams.*

MICKEY *stops a couple of yards from* EDWARD. *He is unsteady and breathing awkwardly.*

EDWARD (*eventually*): Hello, Mickey.

MICKEY: I stopped. (*Pause.*) I stopped takin' the pills.

EDWARD (*pause*): Oh.

MICKEY (*eventually*): I began thinkin' again. Y' see?

EDWARD: Yes . . . well that's . . .

MICKEY: I had to. Start thinkin' again. Even if it had to mean thinkin' about all the bad things. Like . . . like I couldn't even get us a house . . . but you did. Like, I couldn't even get a job, but you gave me one, even though I was useless at it. Even though I'm useless, I had to start thinkin' about them things. Because, because there was one thing left in my life. (*Pause.*) Just one thing I had left, Eddie, Linda an' I wanted to keep her. So . . . so I stopped takin' the pills. But it was too late. D'y' know who tole me about . . . you . . . an' . . . Linda . . . Your mother . . . she came to the factory an' told me.

EDWARD: Mickey, I don't know what she told you but Linda and I are just friends.

MICKEY (*shouts for the first time*): Friends. I could kill you. We were friends weren't we? Blood brothers wasn't it? Remember?

EDWARD: Yes . . . Mickey, I remember.

MICKEY: Well, well how come you got everythin' . . . an' I got nothin'. (*Pause.*) Friends, I've been thinkin' again Eddie. You an' Linda were friends weren't y'? You were friends when she first got pregnant.

EDWARD: Mickey!

MICKEY: Does my child belong to you as well as everythin' else, does she Eddie . . . does she?

EDWARD (*shouts*): No for God's sake!

From the back of the hall we hear a COP *through a loudhailer.*

COP 1: Now listen son, listen to me; I've got armed marksmen with me, but if you do exactly as I say we won't need to use them will we. Now look Michael, put down the gun. Just put the gun down son.

MICKEY (*dismissing their presence*): What am I doin'

here Eddie? I thought I was gonna shoot y'. But I can't even do that. I don't even know if the thing is loaded.

COP 2: What's that woman doin'?

COP 1: Get that woman away . . .

COP 2: Oh shit!

As we see that the MOTHER *has slowly walked down the centre aisle (stalls) towards the platform.*

THE MOTHER: Mickey! Mickey! Don't shoot him Mickey . . .

MICKEY *continues to hold the gun in position.*

MICKEY: Go away Mam . . . Mam you go away from here.

THE MOTHER: No, son.

MICKEY (*shouting as she walks onto the platform*): Mam!

COP 1: You two men move down slowly. I'll get Spencer round the back. Keep down. It looks OK but be careful . . .

THE MOTHER: You had a twin brother. I couldn't afford to keep both of you. His mother couldn't have kids. I agreed to give one of you away!

MICKEY (*something that begins deep down inside him*): You! (*Screaming.*) You. Why didn't you give me away. (*Stands glaring at her, almost uncontrollable with rage.*) I could have been . . . I could have been him!

On the word 'him' he waves at EDWARD *with his gun hand. The gun explodes and blows* EDWARD *apart. He turns to the* COPS *screaming the word 'No' as they open fire and four guns explode, blowing* MICKEY *away. Underscoring begins as* LINDA *runs down the aisle. We hear the* COP *through the loudhailer.*

COP 1: Nobody move, please. It's alright, it's all over, just stay where you are. Spencer . . .

As the light on the scene begins to dim we see the NARRATOR *watching it.*

NARRATOR: And do we blame superstition for what came to pass
Or could it be what we, the English have come to know as class?
Did you ever hear the story of the Johnstone twins,
As like each other as two new pins,

How one was kept and one given away,
How they were born, and they died, on the self same day?

THE END

1. Study the two versions here and then compare them with the final text as it is performed today. Work with someone to make a note of the similarities and differences using a chart with three columns headed Version One, Version Two and Version Three.
2. In groups of four or five prepare performances of the three versions which can be compared and discussed by the whole group.

The themes in the play

1 *Superstition or class*

At the end of the play the Narrator gives us a choice: do we blame superstition or class? Throughout the play he constantly draws our attention to superstition, as for example on p. 8:

There's shoes upon the table an' a joker in the pack,
The salt's been spilled and a looking glass cracked,
There's one lone magpie overhead.

1. Study the rest of the Narrator's speeches and songs and make a list of all the references to superstition.
2. Some directors make the Narrator a dark figure who seems to hover over the action, knowing what is going to happen and almost nudging the characters towards their fate. Make a list of all the references to the devil and fate.
3. Choose one or two of the Narrator's speeches and prepare different performances giving different interpretations, one sympathetic but detached and the other sinister.
4. Using the notes you have made and the performances you have seen, write a piece about the way Willy Russell has

used the idea of a storyteller, the language he gives him and the different ways the role can be interpreted.

2 *I could have been him*

> *Blood Brothers* is a play that could be played like a tennis match with every scene showing first the working-class situation and then a parallel scene showing the middle-class side of it. The only time I allowed myself to do that was in the scene with the policeman. I thought for that tiny scene, if I only did it once, it would be very effective. (Willy Russell)

Study the contrasts that Willy Russell sets up and write about the different life styles and life chances that Eddie and Mickey have. Include such things as:

- the way their parents, both mother and father, treat them
- the language they use
- where they live
- their education
- the way the police treat them
- the work they do
- the power they have

3 *We went dancing*

Dancing is a theme that recurs throughout the play:

p. 44 Mrs Johnstone dances with a picture of the Pope.
p. 46 Mrs Johnstone and Joe dance.
p. 46 Judge: 'And could I take you dancing?'
p. 47 'He's even started dancing, secret dancing.'
p. 47 'Mrs Lyons enters, waltzing with a very awkward fourteen-year-old Edward.'
p. 61 'Edward grabs Linda's mate and begins to waltz her around the street.'
p. 73 'We're goin' dancin'. Right? Then we're goin' for a slap-up meal.'
p. 74 'His mind's gone dancin'.'

p. 78 'That same old tune that always plays, and lets them dance as friends.'

Study the context of each of the above references to dancing. Write down who is involved, what is happening and what happens immediately after. Write a piece entitled 'Dancing in *Blood Brothers*'. You could start:

> Dancing is usually an expression of happiness but sometimes it can be filled with sadness and nostalgia. There is also a tradition in folklore of life being a sinister dance that you get caught up in and cannot escape from. In this essay I will examine how dancing in *Blood Brothers* sometimes symbolises hope and nearly always marks a pleasure that is short lived.

4 *Toy guns and real guns*

> I am just not convinced that banning toy guns will do anything towards curbing the aggression in children. (Willy Russell)

In *Blood Brothers* there are numerous references to guns.

- children play with guns
- there is a fantasy scene where guns become bombs and more and more people get killed
- Edward's father gives him a toy gun
- Edward gives Mickey a toy gun
- Linda asserts her dominance by shooting a pellet gun
- the teenagers fire at the rifle range
- when Eddie and Linda meet to start their romance he mimes the firing of a gun
- Sammy kills during the robbery
- the gun explodes and blows Eddie apart
- four guns explode blowing Mickey away

1. Make notes about the context of each of the above references. Note who is present, who is speaking or doing the significant action, what is the effect of what is said or done and why Willy Russell has included that particular part.

2. Write an essay in three parts showing
   a) how guns are used in *Blood Brothers* and
   b) what your views are on the way our society uses guns
   c) what your views are on the way children play with guns.

5 *Sexier than Marilyn Monroe and living on the never, never*

Most of the characters in *Blood Brothers* dream of attaining happiness and fulfilment by escaping from the life they have at present, but they cannot escape. They're living on the never, never, the devil's at the door, broken bottles are in the sand and there is always a price to pay.

There is a wealth of information about the dreams the characters have. Make notes on each of the following:

p. 6 Mrs Johnstone's husband used to see her as sexier than Marilyn Monroe and leaves her for a girl who looks a bit like Marilyn Monroe.
p. 46 The milkman and the judge both indulge in a male fantasy, seeing Mrs Johnstone as an embodiment of Marilyn Monroe.
p. 11 'If my child was raised in a palace like this one, he wouldn't have to worry where his next meal was comin' from.'
p. 21 'I wish I was our Sammy.'
p. 27 'Darling, I'm sorry, but if, if we can complete this merger, I will, I promise you, have more time.'
p. 35 'There's nothing wrong with my nerves. It's just . . . just this place . . . I hate it. Richard, I don't want to stay here any more. I want to move.'
p. 41 'I wish I could be like . . . my friend.'
p. 42 'Oh bright new day, we're goin' away.'
p. 55 'I wish I was a little bit like that guy.'
p. 65 'If I was the guy . . . we'd while away the hours making future plans.'
p. 71 'You're still a kid. An' I wish I could be as well Eddie.'
p. 77 'The girl would sing the melody but the woman

stands in doubt and wonders what the price would be for letting the young girl out.'

p. 82 'I could have been him!' Is this the final betrayal of the working class or a reasonable desire to escape from its limitations?

1. Use your notes to prepare a talk on 'Dreams in *Blood Brothers*'. You may want to extend the talk by adding a section about your own hopes and dreams.

2. Use the notes you have made or the prompt cards for your talk to write an essay on 'The dreams of the characters in *Blood Brothers*'.

Press reviews

Blood Brothers has always been a play that has received a mixed press. Its simplicity is its strength. Some seem to find a problem with this simplicity as though it makes the play trite or shallow. In my opinion the reverse is true. It's a profoundly moving piece. (Iain McAvoy, company manager at the Phoenix Theatre)

'Willy Scores London Hit', Philip Key, *Liverpool Post and Echo*, 12 April 1983

Willy Russell's musical proved a smash hit in London's West End last night, earning a massive ovation.

There were cheers and five curtain calls for the cast. The Liverpool Playhouse show looks assured of being a big success.

It was also welcomed by theatrical stars in the audience. Andrew Lloyd Webber, composer of *Jesus Christ Superstar*, gave the production a standing ovation with calls of bravo.

And actor Jon Pertwee called it 'The most exciting first night I have attended for years'. He said it was something new to West End audiences by being a melodrama. 'How they will react to a musical melodrama I just don't know but I suspect it will be a marvellous success.'

Willy Russell's musical had a sell-out opening night at the Lyric Theatre on Shaftesbury Avenue, and appeared in a slightly re-written form to the version seen at the Playhouse this year.

Many scenes in the second act have been axed and new ones written in to give stronger emphasis to the conflict between the two mothers, played by Wendy Murray and Barbara Dickson.

And it was Miss Dickson who came across as one of the strongest members of a fine cast with her fine singing voice and tremendous acting ability.

Many in the audience were surprised to learn that it was her first acting role – as she had said in the past, she agreed to it as an old friend of the writer Willy Russell. Her decision was last night proved to be outstandingly a correct one.

But also making strong impressions on last night's audience were George Costigan as the working-class half of the pair of twins and Andrew C. Wadsworth as the other twin brought up in posh surroundings . . .

The critics were last night keeping silent about their views on the play – they will not be known until this morning – but if the audience could write their own reviews they would be giving it raves.

Many of them as they came out of the theatre told me it was one of the most moving yet joyous occasions that they had spent in the theatre.

'Brothers grim', Milton Shulman, *Evening Standard*, 12 April 1983

Blood Brothers at the Lyric is much closer to a folk opera than it is to a musical.

The trouble with folk operas is that in their effort to say something significant about simple people they tend to be earnest and rather dour.

Willy Russell who wrote the book, lyrics and music of *Blood Brothers* is obviously obsessed by the inequities of the English class system.

To make his point that environment is more important than genetics in determining an individual's destiny he has invented a naive fable about twins who are separated at birth because their working-class mother cannot afford to keep both of them . . .

Although no one expects logical or realistic plots in this sort of entertainment what follows is a series of coincidences, unlikely confrontations and pure bathos that puts one in mind of the excesses of the Victorian melodrama.

Whatever the mothers do to keep the twins apart, fate relentlessly drives them together. As the rich boy gravitates hypnotically towards his poor brother and becomes his best friend Mrs Lyons becomes hysterical at the prospect of her secret being discovered.

Willy Russell lays on the class differences that have developed between the twins with the subtlety of a Hyde Park orator.

The well-off boy is neat, speaks posh and is lonely. The poor boy is scruffy, uneducated and friendly. The contrast between the mothers is even more exaggerated – working-class Mum is caring, tolerant and almost saintly while middle-class Mother is selfish, snobbish and neurotic.

It all ends in a hail of bullets when poverty drives poor twin to crime and they quarrel over a girl. It certainly needs some swallowing and it must be conceded that some audiences appear ready to do so.

Relieving this grim tale are some amusing scenes of working-class kids at play and there was a touching sentimentality about the brothers' fondness for each other. Mr Russell's songs are strong and melodic but rather repetitive in mood.

Coda

Blood Brothers is a play with music, not a musical in the traditional sense. The musical content is mainly in song form but there is a deliberate attempt to make the show a filmic experience where the songs carry the narrative forward and the music also heightens the atmosphere.

Rod Edwards is the musical director of the West End production of *Blood Brothers*. He has also been responsible for the productions in Toronto, Australia and New Zealand, on Broadway and the American tour. For those shows he has a supervisory role but at the Phoenix Theatre in London he plays, conducts and is responsible for music cues.

> To play in West End shows and on Broadway requires a very high level of musicianship but *Blood Brothers* also demands empathy from the musicians. In the West End the band has been together for several years with very few changes and you might expect it to be blasé about the show but the opposite is the truth. The play relies on word cues, music cues, scenery cues and lighting cues which means that you have to be one hundred per cent on the ball. An immense amount of work goes into rehearsal so that the show is as smooth as silk. The actors in this show rely on the band for absolute consistency. Every note is written and there is no busking. You might think this would result in a soulless performance but it doesn't. In Toronto we had some top players from *Blood, Sweat and Tears* and *Chicago*. In Dallas we had the best musicians from Nashville and within minutes of the first rehearsal they were enraptured by the show. Here in the West End we have a very compact nine-piece band combining the best of digital technology with excellent live musicians. There are two keyboards and a piano, the drums have an electronic kit as well as a wooden kit and the guitars have pre-programmed effects. The musicians use a computer card which ensures that any effect is exactly the same wherever the show is performed. But in addition we use front-line instruments, trumpets, sax, flute and violin which is great for the folk-feel and the rock-feel of the show. I am always aiming for consistent excellence with the audience at each show feeling that the experience is one that they want to share with others. So far word-of-mouth advertising has been our strongest weapon but you can never be complacent and must always strive for perfection.

Glossary

This glossary is intended for use by overseas readers as well as by English-born readers.

5 *chap* – young man.
six weeks overdue – in the early stages of pregnancy.
we had a do – we had a party.
6 *I was in the club again* – I was pregnant again.
I'm up to here – I've had enough of.
free dinners – school lunches paid for by the state for children in cases of need.
7 *spuds* – potatoes.
the dough – money.
9 *the baby's ticker* – the baby's heart.
dead worried – 'dead' in this sense means 'very'.
the Welfare – the government department that deals with allocating money to families in need and that has the power to take children into care.
10 *being put into care* – the state taking children from a family and looking after them.
11 *effin' and blindin'* – swearing, using obscene language.
12 *piles* – haemorrhoids.
13 *bloody* – a frequently used swearword or expletive; see also 'bleeding'.
14 *you soft get* – a mild term of abuse, 'you stupid man'.
soddin' – an expletive similar to 'bloody'.
19 *rosary* – a string of beads used by Roman Catholics when praying.
20 *robbed me other gun* – stolen my other gun.
hooligan – people who behave in a loud, violent and socially unacceptable way.
21 *but y'can't say nott'n* – you can't say anything (nothing).
22 *nudey women* – naked (nude) women.
he wees – he urinates.

a crate – a box.
gis – Liverpool dialect for 'give us' (me).
23 *are you soft?* – are you stupid?
weed on it – urinated on it.
pissed off – mildly vulgar expression meaning bored or upset.
the 'F' word – the expression used by people who do not want to use the word 'fuck'.
dead mean – very unpleasant.
24 *smashing* – superlative meaning 'excellent'.
25 *y' little robbin' get* – you little thief.
it's last – it's useless.
caps – device for making a toy gun sound like a real gun.
friggin' – a mild and acceptable form of the word 'fucking'.
poshy – a posh person, one who behaves in a refined way.
26 *ta ra* – goodbye.
27 *the bogey man* – a mythological character who is supposed to come for children who misbehave.
28 *hi-ya* – hello.
29 *you're a fuckoff* – Eddie misuses the expression 'fuck off' (a verb) because he does not understand what it means.
30 *bin lid* – the top of a garbage container.
31 *the fastest draw* – as in western films, able to draw a gun from a holster.
hot shot – accurate when shooting.
32 *fingers crossed* – in children's games if you cross your fingers you are safe or you do not mean what you say.
fuck off – generally unacceptable swear word but one which is frequently used in adult literature and films.
youse lot – Liverpool dialect meaning 'you people'.
33 *ciggies* – cigarettes.
half crowns – a coin no longer in circulation, worth 12½p.
34 *his little thingy* – his penis.
37 *Missis* – a working-class way of addressing a woman.
38 *scotch* – whisky.
dock his pocket money – stop his allowance as a punishment.

42 *a summons* – an official notification that you must appear in court.
I never robbed nothin' – I never stole anything.
44 *lardie dah* – posh, refined.
muck – dirt.
46 *probation* – a deferred sentence which means that the criminal has to report to the police regularly.
48 *the dole* – unemployment benefit.
tarrah – goodbye.
49 *a fourpenny scholar* – school children (scholars) are entitled to cheap fares on the buses.
cop shop – police station.
50 *he'll get put away* – he'll be sent to prison.
Oxbridge – the term used to refer to the universities of Cambridge and Oxford.
dorm – dormitory, the place where the students sleep.
51 *flogged* – punished by beating with a cane.
a flying fuck at a rolling doughnut – a piece of calculated vulgarity and insolence that can only result in punishment.
52 *suspended* – banned from school for serious misbehaviour.
54 *taking the piss* – making fun of.
55 *a brace* – an orthodontic device for straightening crooked teeth.
halitosis – a medical condition that results in bad breath.
acne – a medical condition which results in facial spots.
57 *a quid* – a pound coin.
58 *a double bill* – a cinema showing two films.
randy little sods – an exasperated/affectionate expression meaning they are over-preoccupied with sex.
bromide – a substance which if put into tea is supposed to reduce the sexual urges in young men.
59 *a fuckin' head case* – a vulgar but affectionate reference to his mother meaning she is crazy.
61 *naked knockers* – naked breasts.
tits – breasts.
get y' friggin' paws off me – get your hands off me, leave me alone.
62 *a head case* – crazy.

a few bob in your pocket – a small sum of money.
63 *the chippy* – a take-away fish and chip shop.
64 *sweetie pie* – darling.
66 *overtime* – work extra hours.
gonna be on me – I will pay for it.
67 *getting the sack* – being dismissed from your job.
laying people off – making them redundant.
68 *dole office* – where people go to pick up their unemployment benefit.
70 *booze* – alcohol.
the birds – young women.
you're a dick head – you are stupid.
after bein' fucked off – after being refused work.
71 *piss off* – go away.
72 *tart* – vulgar word for girl friend.
the shooters – the guns.
fifty quid – fifty pounds.
fifty notes – fifty pounds.
73 *a slap-up meal* – a first-class meal.
don't piss about with me – don't delay in doing what I tell you to do.
74 *sent him down* – sent him to prison.
life – life sentence.
75 *he's been out* – he's been released from prison.
76 *the housin' committee* – the committee that allocates cheap rented housing to people who need it.
80 *he's callin' your number up* – fate decrees you will die.